The Face of Privatization in Pakistan

Ghulam Samad • Naseem Faraz

The Face of Privatization in Pakistan

palgrave
macmillan

Ghulam Samad
Chief Research Division
CAREC Institute
Urumqi, China

Naseem Faraz
Pakistan Institute of Development
Economics
Islamabad, Pakistan

ISBN 978-981-97-8384-7 ISBN 978-981-97-8385-4 (eBook)
https://doi.org/10.1007/978-981-97-8385-4

This Palgrave Macmillan imprint is published by the registered company Springer Nature Singapore Pte Ltd.
The registered company address is: 152 Beach Road, #21-01/04 Gateway East, Singapore 189721, Singapore

Preface

Pakistan is facing deep macro-fiscal challenges of persistent high fiscal deficit and debt stress. The fragile health of state-owned enterprises (SOEs) remains a key factor playing its role in piling up public debt and continued burden on the nation's fiscal resources. The heavy economic losses coupled with subsidies, contingent liabilities, and grants to keep them operational has become a consistent fiscal wrath for the Government of Pakistan.

In the 1950s and 1960s, a golden era of high economic growth, country observed growing disparities in distribution of income, led to large share of asset holding in the hands of 22 families. The government has taken policy decision in the 1970s to bring the fundamental change in the economic policy by nationalizing the private sector. This policy decision was to curb the accumulation of wealth in particular businesses and families. However, the nationalization strategy did not yield the expected economic gains. In later years, results of policy showed that, at one hand, it had a regressive effect on the income distribution, while on the other hand, this policy led to a significant increase in the fiscal burden as the government was forced to bail out these struggling entities with taxpayers' money. In the following decade, this resulted in a large fiscal deficit (around 8%) in late the 1980s and government left with no choice to start reversal of the nationalization of entities.

In late the 1980s when economy grappled with high fiscal deficit and debt payments, to deal with the bad economic conditions, the government has obtained IMF's Structural Adjustment Program. To accomplish the IMF conditionalities, the privatization of SOEs program had begun in 1990s with the aim to revive the private sector through deregulation and disinvestment.

The SOEs reforms were aimed to reduce fiscal stress and encourage an efficient and competitive economic environment in the country. However, the privatization program in Pakistan has sparked a heated debate, with arguments being presented by both its advocates and critics. Due to the lack of consensus, there is a need of an impartial assessment of the current state of SOEs and the effects of privatization without any ideological bias.

The privatization was started and a large number of SOEs had privatized in different phases. In the first phase, the government offered 108 PSEs out of a total of 167 for privatization. In less than 18 months, 66 had been privatized, leaving 42 for the second phase. The government privatized two of the five large national banks and initiated measures to sell some of the major infrastructure facilities, telecommunications, and energy sectors in the next phase. During 2002–2008, the government continued to privatize the units in the infrastructure, energy, and engineering sector. Further, 63 PSEs had been privatized during this phase. Currently, around 212 SOEs are operating in various sectors of Pakistan within which 85 SOEs are commercial, 44 non-commercial SOEs, and 83 subsidiaries of the commercial SOEs. After 2008, the government initiated a fresh program of privatization, which aims at privatizing more than 49 units till 2023.

Though the privatization program was aimed at reducing the government's fiscal burden, improving the efficiency and competitiveness of SOEs. However, the program faced significant challenges as well as criticism, including political interference, corruption, lack of transparency, and opposition from labor unions and other stakeholders. This book offers an in-depth examination of the present state of SOEs in various sectors to sensitize the importance of privatization in Pakistan. Turning to main objective of the book, it provides detail assessment of the privatization of SOEs by covering the operational, financial, economic, and social dimensions involved. To achieve these objectives, this study has been systematically divided into distinct sections.

Part I of the book presents a detailed historical perspective that provides understanding of the development of privatization program over time. It provides an insightful discussion on several stylized facts related to different phases of privatization, including transactions across various sectors and resulting proceeds. To enrich our comprehension further, global stylized facts pertaining to privatization are also explored within this section. It has been concluded that market environment dynamics played an important role in determining success or failure along with other factors like fair process and institutional framework.

Moreover, in this part, it sheds light on the financial landscape of SOEs, operating across various sectors in Pakistan. It includes information on net profits, losses, and employment in the financial sector, Industrial and Engineering sector, Manufacturing and Mining sector, Services sector, Oil and Gas sector, Power sector, Infrastructure and Transportation sector, as well as Trading and Marketing sector. The report also conducts a detailed analysis of the fiscal burden incurred by SOEs within these sectors. The primary focus remains on assessing subsidies granted along with grants issued which had been distributed amongst each industry analyzed under this study. Investigation revealed that large-scale industries like Power and Energy sector received substantial subsidies but incurred significant losses during 2018–2019. On the other hand, Oil and Gas sector proved to be highly profitable without any subsidies.

Part II of this study presents an exploratory analysis of the performance, efficiency, and competitiveness of the SOEs before and after privatization which reveals that most sectors are not performing at par. The main indicators include sales, assets, net profit to sales ratio, rate of return, sales to employment ratio, and concentration ratios. An overall analysis reveals that privatization has not resulted in any significant improvement in the listed indicators. In order to get a more insightful picture, the same analysis has been repeated for sector-wise and firm-wise SOEs. The results depict that except for Oil and Gas sector, Financial sector, and firms in the Miscellaneous category, all the other sectors are performing low in terms of rate of return (ROR) and profit-to-sale ratio. Oil and Gas sector has proved to be the most efficient followed by Power sector. The lowest efficiency has been shown by Manufacturing and Engineering sector.

In order to complement the exploratory analysis, *Part II* of the book also presents an empirical investigation of the post-privatization performance and efficiency of non-financial SOEs in various sectors in Pakistan. An econometric approach has been adopted for this empirical assessment. The results show that firms show a slight improvement in productivity after privatization, however, this improvement is not statistically significant. Contrary to that, the efficiency (measured by return on assets) of the privatized firms increased significantly as compared to their government-owned counter-parts. However, efficiency through the increase in sales does not show any improvement. The analysis has also investigated the role of democratic government and donor's conditionality on the privatization decisions. The results reveal that both the factors hold no significant impact on privatization decisions.

In *Part III* of the book, we reviewed the case studies of major privatizations in the history of Pakistan. The analysis of key players before and after privatization revealed several findings. While some industries, like cement, were consistently profitable prior to privatization, others faced challenges. In case of KESC, no significant increase in the generation capacity of KE has been noticed over a period of 17 years. The net profit/loss scenario was also not much satisfying. Maple Leaf Cement (MLCF) incurred losses despite previous success. PTCL, with its impressive pre-privatization track record, may not have been a suitable candidate for divestment. ABL's uncertain past performance improved after privatization, though NPL ratio post-privatization remained high. Limited historical data on HBL made it difficult to assess its pre-privatization state, but post-privatization results showed significant improvement.

In order to ensure transparency and effectiveness of the privatization process, there is a need of a well-designed legal framework. *Part IV* of this book provides a comprehensive overview of the legal framework of privatization in Pakistan, including a critical analysis of the laws and regulations governing the process, the role of regulatory bodies, and the legal protection available to investors. The legal framework includes SOEs (Governance and Operations) Act, 2023, and Privatization Commission Ordinance, 2000. It has been observed that these laws have been silent on certain aspects including post-privatization procedures of the privatized SOEs.

In addition to the legal framework for privatization, *Part IV* also examines the role of Public-Private Partnerships (PPPs) in supporting sustainable and inclusive economic growth in Pakistan. It explores the history, legal and regulatory framework, types, case studies, challenges, and potential benefits of PPPs in Pakistan. The discussion highlights the importance of developing strong institutional and regulatory frameworks, ensuring transparency and accountability, and capacity building within the public sector to ensure the success of PPPs in Pakistan. The book concludes that PPPs can be an important tool for leveraging private sector investment, expertise, and innovation to support the delivery of critical infrastructure and services in Pakistan, but their success depends on addressing the challenges and investing in the necessary institutional and regulatory frameworks.

The decision to initiate the privatization of state-owned enterprises was driven by several factors, such as reducing fiscal burden, boosting economic growth, attracting foreign investment, and enhancing efficiency. However, this process was influenced heavily by political pressures, interest groups' agendas and rent-seeking behavior leading to undesired entities being privatized while necessary ones were not, Therefore, *Part V* of this book explores the privatization of several key public institutions which were highly politicized, including Pakistan Steel Mills, United Bank Limited, Muslim Commercial Bank, Pakistan International Airlines, and DISCOs.

In order to reap up the benefits of privatization, the first and foremost requirement is to identify the actual need of privatization. Overall, this book offers a valuable contribution to the debate on the fate of SOEs in Pakistan and the potential solutions for improving their performance. It is an essential reading for policymakers, scholars, and anyone interested in the economic development of Pakistan.

Urumqi, China
Islamabad, Pakistan

Ghulam Samad
Naseem Faraz

Acknowledgment

We extend our deepest gratitude to the esteemed experts whose invaluable discussions and comments on the first draft have made this book, *Face of Privatization in Pakistan*, possible. We have benefited immensely from their insights. We are grateful to Haroon Sharif, former Federal Minister, Board of Investment, for his profound insights into privatization and deep understanding of the subject. Our thorough discussions with Wajid Rana, former Federal Secretary, helped in shaping the detailed content on SOEs and privatized SOEs. The detailed discussions with Ahmad Qadir, Director General of the Competition Commission of Pakistan, enriched our knowledge of competition issue. We also thank Mr. Zafar Iqbal Sobani, Member of the Privatization Commission of Pakistan, for his practical insights, which enhanced our understanding of competition and privatization policy in Pakistan. Dr. Khaqan Babar, Additional Secretary of the Privatization Commission of Pakistan, provided dedicated support on this subject. Muhammad Arif Sargana, Director at the Pakistan Telecommunication Authority, shared his technical expertise on the telecommunication sector. Finally, our heartiest thanks go to Dr. Ishrat Hussain, former governor of the State Bank of Pakistan, for his economic insights on financial institutions, and Shamsul Mulk, former Chief Minister of Khyber Pakhtunkhwa, for his seasoned perspective on the power sector in Pakistan. Their collective wisdom and input have significantly enriched this book, providing a comprehensive view of privatization in Pakistan. We are immensely grateful for their time, effort, and the wealth of knowledge they have shared with us. Finally, we would like to express our sincere thanks to Ms. Aisha Irum for their invaluable research assistance in the completion of this research.

Contents

Abbreviations

ABL	Allied Bank Limited
ADB	Asian Development Bank
AKFED	Agha Khan Fund for Economic Development
APCMA	Pakistan Cement Manufacturers Association
BQPS	Bin Qasim Power Station
CP	Commercial Paper
DFIs	Development Finance Institutions
DGKC	Dera Ghaz Khan Cement
DISCOs	Distribution Companies
GoP	Government of Pakistan
HBL	Habib Bank Limited
IFC	International Finance Corporation
IMF	International Monetary Fund
KESC	Karachi Electric Supply Corporation
KE	K-electric
KMLG	Kohinoor Mills Limited Group
KWH	Kilowatt per hour
MCB	Muslim Commercial Bank
MLCFL	Maple Leaf Cement Factory Limited
MLEC	Maple Leaf Electric Company Limited
NBP	National Bank of Pakistan
NCBs	Nationalized Commercial Banks
NEPRA	National Electric Power Regulatory Authority
NPL	Non-Performing Loans
O&M	Operating and Management
PBC	Pakistan Banking Council
PEMRA	Pakistan Electronic Media Regulatory Authority

PIA	Pakistan International Airlines
PIDC	Pakistan Industrial Development Corporation
PPPs	Public-Private Partnerships
PSCs	Public Sector Enterprises
PTA	Pakistan Telecommunication Authority
PTCL	Pakistan Telecommunication Limited
PTDC	Pakistan Tourism Development Corporation
PTVC	Pakistan Television Corporation Limited
PWC	PriceWaterhouseCoopers
SAP	Structural Adjustment Program
SBP	State Bank of Pakistan
SOEs	State-owned Enterprises
SSGC	Sui Southern Gas Company
SCCP	State Cement Corporation of Pakistan
T&D	Transmission and Distribution Losses
ROE	Return on Equity
ROR	Rate of Return
UBL	United Bank Limited
WAPDA	Water and Power Development Authority
WCIL	White Cement Industries Limited
WPIDC	West Pakistan Industrial Development Corporation
YoY	Year on Year
ZTBL	Zarai Taraqiati Bank Limited

List of Figures

List of Tables

List of Boxes

CHAPTER 1

Introduction

Abstract This book offers a comprehensive assessment of privatization of state-owned enterprises (SOEs) in Pakistan, initiated in the 1990s as part of the IMF's Structural Adjustment Program. Government was aimed at reducing the high fiscal burden through privatization proceeds, this policy sought to enhance efficiency and economic growth. During past three decades, privatization has been implemented across important sectors such as telecommunications, energy, and finance. This privatization process has sparked an intense debate, with criticisms focusing on performance of privatized SOEs, potential job losses, political gain, and reduced access to essential services for the poorer segments of society. The book delves into a data-driven examination of the privatization outcomes, exploring the operational, financial, and socio-economic effects across various sectors. It argues for a balanced approach that neither fully embraces nationalization nor aggressive privatization. It suggests the adoption of Public-Private Partnerships (PPPs) as a viable alternative to improve efficiency while maintaining strategic control over essential services. This scholarly work aims to contribute significantly to the discourse on economic reform and governance in Pakistan, offering a path forward that could influence future policy decisions and economic stability in the region.

G. Samad, N. Faraz, *The Face of Privatization in Pakistan*,
https://doi.org/10.1007/978-981-97-8385-4_1

Keywords Macroeconomic challenges • SOE inefficiencies • Privatization program • Fiscal deficit • Public-Private partnerships • Regulatory framework

Pakistan's economy has grappled with severe macroeconomic challenges, which have pushed the country to the brink of default in the recent past. With declining economic growth, the fiscal deficit is widening over time. The poor performance of SOEs has become a significant contributor to the country's financial difficulties. The inefficiencies of SOEs require continuous financial support and bailouts from the government, which, on one hand, burden taxpayers due to the application of new taxes to increase revenue, and on the other hand, reduce the funds available for important public service delivery, leading to increased demand for public debt.

To address the financial woes, the Government of Pakistan sought for the IMF's Structural Adjustment Program in the 1990s, among others, which conditioned the privatization of SOEs. This initiative marked the beginning of Pakistan's privatization program Sadiq et al. (2020), Salman & Ali (2022), Yar et al. (2013). The main goal of the privatization was to reduce the fiscal load on the government's treasury by shifting ownership and management to the private sector, thereby increasing competition and improving operational efficiency Ahmad (1999). Since then, over the three decades, the progress on privatization unfolded gradually, highly influenced by government priorities, economic conditions, and strategic factors. Prominent sectors have been considered for privatization included telecommunications, energy, financial institutions, manufacturing, and the industrial sector Khan (2009), Mustafa et al. (2023).

Since the beginning of the SOEs privatization in Pakistan, an intense debate sparked among various groups. Some advocate for aggressive privatization measures while others express concerns. Critics of privatization center their criticisms around the following main issues: First, labor unions strictly criticize the privatization stance due to fears of potential job losses, changes in working conditions, and perceived threats to workers' rights. These concerns have led to protests, strikes, and demonstrations against privatization attempts. Second, political actors have also used privatization as a platform to advance their agendas for voters gain. Third, critics argue that privatizing sectors like healthcare, education, or utilities might lead to reduced affordability or exclusion of marginalized populations. Finally, the performance of several privatized SOEs remains a concern due to poor outcomes in the post-privatization period.

In light of these concerns about privatization from various circles, it is important to provide a well-informed perspective on the actual effects of privatization. Given the lack of comprehensive data-based empirical analysis, there is a need for rigorous and evidence-based assessment of the privatization of SOEs. This book aims to fill that gap by providing a comprehensive examination of privatized SOEs, shedding light on its historical context, SOEs financial landscapes, performance evaluations, case studies, legal frameworks, and the role of public-private partnerships (PPPs).

The rigor of this book lies in the following key contributions: First, it moves beyond subjective discussions to build its analysis on a solid research methodology, using detailed financial statements from SOEs to assess their performance before and after privatization. Second, it deepens the discussion by exploring case studies from four critical sectors: finance, cement, power, and telecommunications. Finally, it addresses potential improvements to the privatization model in Pakistan, proposing directions for future enhancements.

This book makes argument that it is imperative to find a balanced approach, advocating neither for nationalization or unabated privatization. This balanced approach can be in the form of (PPPs) or efficient privatization approach which can potentially enable the government to maintain control over strategic sectors while benefiting from private sector efficiency and investment as well.

Pakistan needs a comprehensive privatization policy and a well-designed and unbiased legal and regulatory framework that must guarantees a successful privatization program. In this regard, Privatization Commission and Privatization Commission Ordinance, 2000, are the main pillars of the legal and regulatory framework of privatization in Pakistan. However, our review of the Ordinance shows that one of the major reasons behind not getting the intended results from the privatization program is its weak design and implementation. Thus, there is a need of an unbiased regulators whose job is to identify the necessary privatization and also monitor the post-privatization performance.

Privatization and public sector reforms are dynamic processes influenced by evolving economic, political, and social factors. As such, the insights generated by this research are not only relevant in the present context but also have long-term implications for policy formulation and decision-making. By examining the contemporary relevance of privatization in Pakistan and its potential implications for future economic development, the book ensures its enduring value in the realm of public policy and governance.

The organization of chapters in this book reflects a logical progression, starting with a historical overview and global insights, followed by an analysis of the financial landscapes, performance evaluations, case studies, and legal frameworks. Each chapter is carefully written to offer valuable insights and recommendations for policymakers, scholars, and anyone interested in Pakistan's economic development. By exploring the successes, failures, and lessons learned from past privatization experiences, this book aims to contribute to the ongoing debate on the fate of SOEs in Pakistan and the potential solutions for improving their performance.

References

Ahmad, E. (1999). Retiring public debt through privatization. *Pakistan Journal of Applied Economics, 15*(1–2), 1–18.

Khan, M. Z. (2009). Liberalization and economic crisis in Pakistan. *Rising to the Challenge in Asia: A Study of Financial Markets: Asian Development Bank, 9.*

Mustafa, S., Zafar, A., Naeem, M., Hasan, M., & Rabbani, M. F. (2023). Economic instabilities lead to privatization in any state, an exposition of Pakistan's privatization policy. *Journal of Positive School Psychology*, 678–692.

Sadiq, N., Laila, U., Mehmood, T., & Haqqi, T. R. (2020). Privatization of national assets: Solution to fiscal deficits. *Journal of Accounting and Finance in Emerging Economies, 6*(3), 897–904.

Salman, A., & Ali, B. (2022). The IMF stabilization program and macroeconomic analysis for Pakistan. *IPRI policy paper.*

Yar, A., Sarawak, M., & Arif-Affendi, M. (2013). Privatization and fiscal deficit: A case study of Pakistan. *Research Journal of Finance and Accounting, 4*(14), 1–10.

PART I

Privatization in Pakistan

CHAPTER 2

Privatization Trends

Abstract The privatization process in Pakistan from a regulated to a market-oriented economy has spanned over a period of three decades. This chapter offers insight on the historical context of this economic policy shifts, emphasizing on the transition from nationalization in the 1970s to extensive reforms in the 1990s. It also outlines three distinct phases of privatization, from aggressive disinvestment and regulatory reforms in the 1990s to continued divestment efforts post-2008. While privatization has led to revenue boosts in sectors like energy and telecommunications, challenges such as unit closures post-privatization have hindered sustainable growth. Moreover, global examples underscore the diverse outcomes of privatization, emphasizing the need for context-specific approaches and robust regulatory frameworks.

Keywords Privatization history • Development policy • Nationalization strategy • Market-based economy • Privatization efforts

Privatization in Pakistan: Some Stylized Facts

The development policy in Pakistan has taken major reversal in assigning the relative role to public and private sectors in last 30 years. Extensive efforts were made to transform the system from an over-regulated system to a more open and market-oriented economy. Since the beginning of

G. Samad, N. Faraz, *The Face of Privatization in Pakistan*, https://doi.org/10.1007/978-981-97-8385-4_2

privatization in 1991, more than 194 public-sector enterprises (PSEs) have been privatized (1991–2021) to correct fiscal and macroeconomic imbalances. Government earned around $11 billion from the sales of PSEs. However, anecdotal evidence suggests that the fundamental change in economic policy always did not end up with perceived economic gains. A considerable controversy remains on the success and failure of privatization of the public sector enterprises (PSEs) in Pakistan.

In the beginning of 1970s, a serious concern had been shown on the unequal income distribution and concentration of income in the hands of the 22 families, making them too rich at the cost of the poor segment of the population. This issue dominated the election of the 1970. From 1972 to 1977, the government brought about a fundamental change in the economic policy and expanded the role of public sector by nationalizing the private sector. However, this nationalization strategy did not yield the expected economic gains later. It had a regressive effect on the income distribution, the concentration of the economic power in a few hands and the inadequate distribution of benefits to the "bottom 40%" of the population. This policy was reversed after the large surge in fiscal deficit in late 1980s (Husain, 2004).

The 1990s had gone down as a major milestone in terms of privatization in the economic history of Pakistan. The economy underwent extensive changes in the economic management within a short period of two years in the first half of that decade. Significant efforts were made to transform the system from an over-regulated and inward-looking system into a more open, deregulated, and market-oriented economy. Figure 2.1 shows the total number of privatization transactions till 2021. It shows that the largest number of transactions occurred in 1992. Table 2.1 also shows sector-wise privatization proceeds till 2021 where the highest amount of privatization proceeds were earned from the capital markets (303 billion rupees) followed by telecommunication sector (187 billion rupees).

Phases of Privatization in Pakistan

The history of privatization in Pakistan is characterized by three distinct phases, each with its own set of objectives and strategies. The first phase dates back to the 1960s when the government aimed at fostering a strong private sector by creating opportunities for entrepreneurs to flourish. This initial period was marked by significant efforts toward deregulation and liberalization policies that would enable greater private investment. The

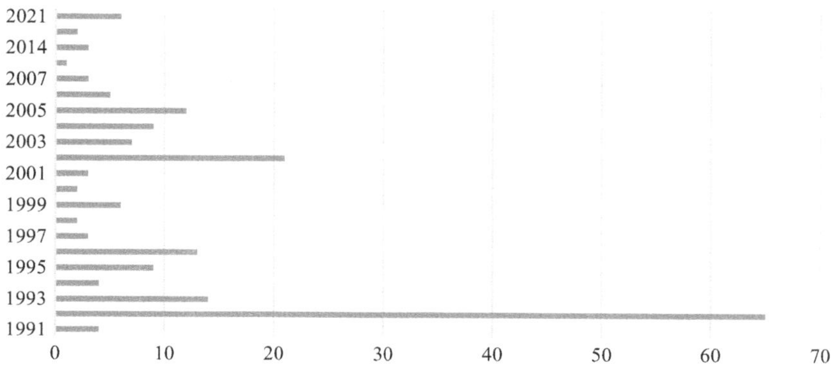

Fig. 2.1 Number of Privatization Transactions (1991–2021). (*Source*: Privatization Commission of Pakistan)

Table 2.1 Sector-wise Transaction Proceeds

Sector	*No of transactions*	*Proceeds/Billion PKR*
Banking	7	41.02
Capital markets	26	303.5
Energy	15	54.3
Telecoms	4	187.36
Automobiles	7	1.10
Cements	17	16.18
Chemical/fertilizer	23	41.92
Engineering	7	0.18
Ghee mills	24	0.84
Mineral	1	0.006
Rice and roti plants	23	0.33
Textiles	4	0.37
Newspapers	5	0.27
Tourism	4	1.81
Sale of Public Properties	6	0.14
Miscellaneous	5	0.15
Total	178	649

Source: Privatization Commission of Pakistan, 2023.

second phase began in the 1990s as part of an ambitious plan to reduce fiscal losses through disinvestment and regulatory reforms. Under this framework, around two-thirds (108) out of a total of 167 public-sector enterprises were offered up for privatization within just 18 months; leaving only 42 left for further consideration under the third phase. The following years from 2002 up until 2008 saw continued efforts by the government toward divesting its holdings within infrastructure units, energy resources, and engineering services—an endeavor that ultimately brought about significant change within these respective industries. A total of 63 PSEs had been privatized during this phase.

The government's commitment toward this policy had been further evident through its fresh program initiated post-2008 which aimed at privatizing more than 49 units until 2023.[1] A detailed analysis of Fig. 2.1 reveals how these transactions have evolved since 1991. However, what sets this current wave apart from previous ones is that it promised to not just raise revenues but also enhance operational efficiencies in the previously inefficient PSEs. This resulted in an impressive Rs. 655 billion being earned, which equates to approximately US$11 billion[2] when converted using exchange rates for their respective years. To ascertain this figure, we calculated revenues from PSEs sales and ensured that it accurately reflected fluctuations caused by varying exchange rates over time.

Privatization Achievements

The non-financial sector has experienced a significant boost in revenues, with the privatization of the energy, cement, fertilizer, and telecom sectors contributing to almost two-thirds of the total earnings as depicted in Fig. 2.2. This remarkable growth was primarily witnessed during the third phase (2002–2008). Prior to privatization however, public sector enterprises (PSEs) were granted tax exemptions along with subsidies and grants from the government that had a direct impact on their profit margins. It is noteworthy that since then there had been noticeable reductions in tax exemption rates and subsidies given to PSEs which significantly increased overall revenue generation while also helping reduce fiscal deficits (Fig. 2.3).

Upon examining the post-privatization facts in Pakistan, it is apparent that both the public and private sectors experienced significant failures.

[1] https://www.thenews.com.pk/print/440589-govt-to-privatise-49-public-sector-concerns

[2] We have calculated this amount by multiplying the revenues from PSEs with the exchange rate in the respective years.

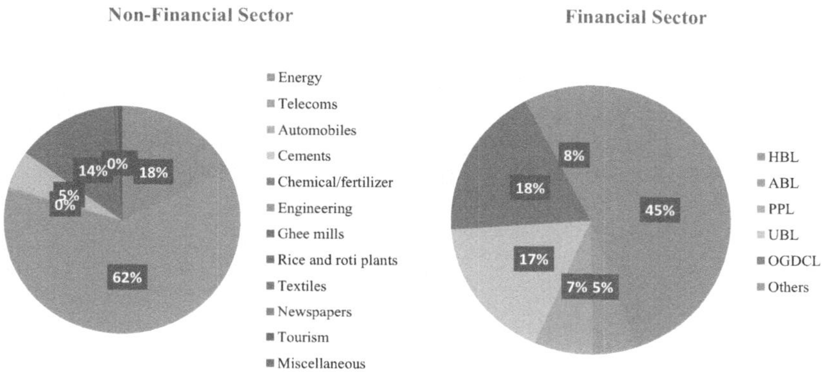

Fig. 2.2 Sector-wise Share of Privatization Proceeds (1992–2021). (*Source*: Privatization Commission of Pakistan)

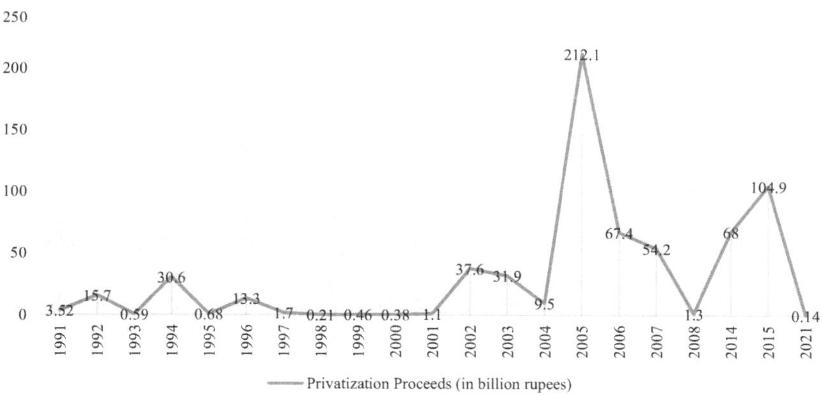

Fig. 2.3 Privatization Proceeds by GoP 1991–2021 (in billion rupees). (*Source*: Privatization Commission of Pakistan)

The closure of over 16 privatized units (as seen in Box 2.1) during this period had a devastating impact on the economy. In fact, such closures were responsible for impeding industrial and economic growth rates following the first phase of privatization. The repercussions of these unit closures have been far-reaching, posing considerable challenges to key industries across Pakistan. Consequently, there had been a noticeable

Box 2.1 Units Closed after Privatization
Naya Daur Motors, Zeal Pak Cement. National Cement, General Refractories, Pak PVC, Swat Elutriation, Nowshera PVC, Nowshera Chemicals, Hydari Veg Ghee, Karachi Pipe Mills, Dandot Cement, Pak China Fertilizer, Metropolitan Steel, Pak Switchgear, Quality Steel, Indus Steel Pipe, Fazal Veg. Ghee, Haripur Veg. Oil, Khyber Veg, Suraj Ghee Indus

hindrance to sustainable development efforts as well as limitations placed on future investment opportunities within various sectors. Thus, while initial plans may indicate success through government divestment strategies—which aims at promoting innovation and competition—reality reflects how factors like weak regulatory frameworks can be detrimental if not addressed comprehensively beforehand.

Privatization: Global Stylized Facts

While presenting cases and examples from various regions across the globe to highlight the effectiveness of privatization policies in driving progress and fostering growth, it is important to consider that this policy may not be suitable for every country and context. There have been instances where privatization has led to increased inequality and job losses, particularly in developing nations with weak regulatory frameworks. Thus, it is essential to take into account differences in political systems, cultural values, and economic conditions before advocating for a blanket implementation of privatization policy. Ultimately, a context-specific approach is necessary to determine whether or not privatization can be a beneficial policy for a particular country or region.

The impact of privatization on the global economy has been significant, as evidenced by Fig. 2.4 which highlights a staggering $1.3 trillion in total privatization proceeds since 2010. This represents a dramatic increase compared to the previous decade and shows a growing trend toward market-driven policies that prioritize private ownership over state control (Government of Pakistan, 2023).

When examining developing nations like China, it becomes clear how influential this shift has been. In fact, China has consistently been ranked among the top countries for privatization since 2009—cementing its position as a major player in this arena. Specifically, China was not only the largest privatizer worldwide back in 2009 but also secured first place in 2013 and 2014 as well, showcasing its commitment to leveraging private enterprise for economic growth and expansion on an international scale.

Over the course of five years, from 2007 to 2012, approximately half of the state-owned enterprises globally were privatized. Furthermore, in South Asia alone there was a significant amount of privatization observed between 2000 and 2008 with proceeds totaling $17.45 billion—the majority being realized in India at an astounding rate of 55%, followed closely by Pakistan's contribution of 43%. The remaining countries including Afghanistan, Bangladesh, Nepal, and Sri Lanka contributed only 2% collectively (as seen on Fig. 2.4). It is worth noting that major industries targeted for such changes have been primarily within infrastructure sector like energy production as well as financial or manufacturing entities, all experiencing impressive levels off expansion due to these shifts toward private ownership structures Khan (2003), (World Bank Privatization Database).

The practice of privatization has become increasingly prevalent not just in the developing countries, but also among developed nations. The United Kingdom alone witnessed a substantial increase in privatization proceeds, from $7.8 billion to $17.2 billion between 2009 and 2014, respectively. In the wake of the global recession that hit after 2008, European governments resorted to increasing their rates of privatization as a means to mitigate their financial deficits. Such measures have yielded positive results with EU's total proceeds reaching an impressive $68.0

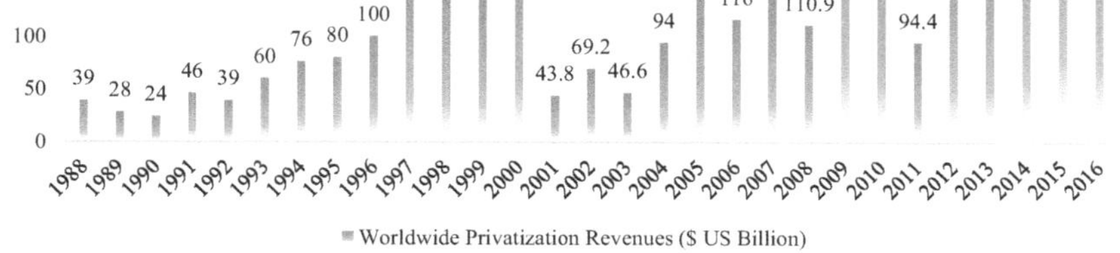

Fig. 2.4 Worldwide Privatization Revenues 1988–2016 ($ US Billion). (*Source*: Privatization Barometer Report 1988–2016)

billion in 2013; this figure further increased to reach $77.6 billion by the year following—topping off at approximately one-third of all global annual totals recorded for that same year. These figures demonstrate how significant such moves are toward boosting economies and addressing government deficits during financially difficult times experienced on both national and international levels alike—indeed highlighting how crucial it is for any country wanting sustainable economic growth over time! (Privatization Barometer Report, 2015 (Meginson, 2016)) (Fig. 2.5).

Despite privatization both in the developed and developing countries, prior evidence suggest that privatization did not lead to achieve the economic gains unanimously across the countries. Privatization has had largely positive effects on the economic and financial performance of the companies involved. This process was also a wider source of spillover benefits such as the technological diffusion from foreign ownership of former PSEs. Moreover, privatization programs frequently achieved additional objectives, including the generation of revenues to relax state budget constraints and a broadening of share ownership amongst the population (Estrin & Pelletier, 2018).

In contrast, the lesson was not always common in developing countries. The consequences of privatization shows that the success of privatization depends on the market environment, fair process, and institutuonal environment. If the mode of privatization is inappropriate or the market

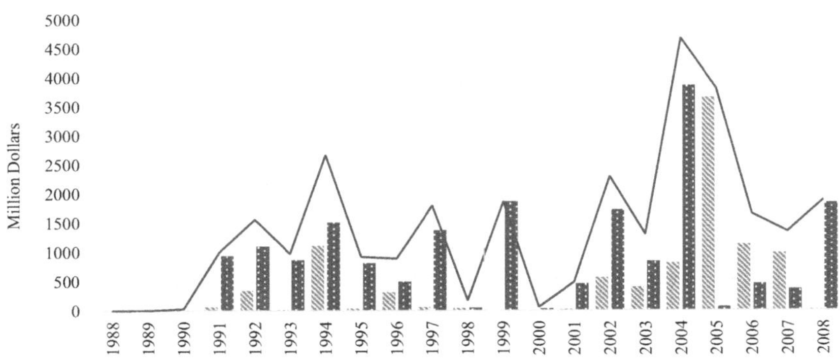

Fig. 2.5 Privatization in South Asian Region. (*Source*: World Bank Privatization survey)

environment is not competitive, privatization does not enhance the performance of the firms involved (Estrin et al., 2009). Moreover, privatization programs in the developing countries had been associated with scandals as well. The political interference led to inappropriate valuations that caused extreme wealth inequalities. In short, trends in privatization suggest that privatzation is not unique to Pakistan, it is equally happening in both developed and developing countries. However, the consequences of privatization vary greatly across the countries.

References

Estrin, S., Hanousek, J., Kocenda, E., & Svejnar, J. (2009). The effects of privatization and ownership in transition economies. *Journal of Economic Literature, 47*(3), 699–728.

Estrin, S., & Pelletier, A. (2018, February). Privatization in developing countries: What are the lessons of recent experience? *The World Bank Research Observer, 33*(1), 65–102.

Government of Pakistan (2023). *Completed transactions*, Privatization Commission. https://privatisation.gov.pk/Detail/NTU0ZjE1NGQtNmYzNC00NWZjLWIxZTEtYWMzMzliYzFhNzk4

Husain, I. (2004, April). Policy considerations before bank privatization country experience. In *World Bank, IMF and Brookings Instituion conference on Role of State-owned Financial Instituions Policy and Practice, April* (pp. 26–27).

Khan, I. A. (2003). Impact of privatization on employment and output in Pakistan. *Pakistan Development Review, 42*(4), 513–536. https://doi.org/10.30541/v42i4IIpp.513-536

Meginson, Willam, (2016). Privatization Barometer Report, 2015, University of Oklahoma,and King Fahd University of Petroleum and Minerals.

CHAPTER 3

Current State of State-owned Enterprises in Pakistan

Abstract The SOEs are frequently criticized for inefficiencies and poor performance. Pakistan is not an exception, the SOEs are facing challenges of mismanagement, overstaffing, and high debt. This chapter presents a detailed overview on the financial status of SOEs, covering revenue generation, net profit/loss, reliance on subsidies, and public debt. The findings reveal that some sectors impose a significant fiscal burden, while others, like oil and gas, are profitable. In this chapter, we also examine efficiency through sales to employment ratios across sectors to identify opportunities for optimal restructuring. The analysis highlights the need for efficiency improvements, as many sectors show low rates of return and profitability.

Keywords Fiscal imbalances • Debt stress • State-Owned Enterprises (SOEs) • Public debt • Subsidies • Contingent liabilities • Government grants

SOEs, in the developing world, often face criticism for their inefficiencies and poor operational performance. These inefficiencies can manifest in various forms, such as mismanagement, overstaffing, costly investments, high debt, fiscal burden, poor quality service, and corruption. Likewise, SOEs in Pakistan have been plagued by inefficiencies and poor

G. Samad, N. Faraz, *The Face of Privatization in Pakistan*,
https://doi.org/10.1007/978-981-97-8385-4_3

policymaking, resulting in loss-making entities that contribute to government debt. As of 2021 the total outstanding domestic debt and liabilities of the SOEs were more than 1.67 trillion PKR. This is an increase of almost 2% as compared to the same period in the year 2020. This accounts for almost 2.7% of the GDP. The largest part of these liabilities are owed to Pakistan International Airlines (PIA), which is 156.4 billion PKR, followed by Water and Power Development Authority (WAPDA) with 76.6 billion PKR.

The large SOEs losses force government to provide heavy-sized equity injection, subsidies, grants, loans, and guarantees on loans for improving their operational efficiency and service delivery. As of 2019, the total amount of subsidies given to the SOEs amounts to 203 billion PKR. However, it is mostly debated that these guaranteed subsidies being provided by the government to the SOEs have not only distorted competition but also decreased the social innovation that could have been the outcome of this investment if utilized strategically.

The increasing subsidies and liabilities indicate an alarming state of SOEs which may escalate in future to cause severe repercussions for the economy, if left unaddressed. To better understand the financial status of SOEs in Pakistan and their potential for privatization, it is important to examine in detail the key financial statistics of SOEs over the years such as revenue generation, net profit/loss, and fiscal burden in the form of subsidies and public debt.

State-owned enterprises (SOEs) in Pakistan are categorized into Public Sector Companies (PSCs), Development Finance Institutions (DFIs), and federal authorities. PSCs are further classified as either commercial or non-commercial entities. In 2013–2014, there were 130 SOEs operating in Pakistan, which increased to 138 by 2016–2017. The SOEs began incurring losses in 2016, and despite a surge in overall revenues (Fig. 3.3), these revenues were insufficient to cover operational costs. This situation increased dependence of SOEs on government subsidies, which is a large size subsidy and becoming a fiscal burden on the national exchequer.

As a result, the government started privatizing smaller units while retaining a significant portion of assets. According to recent data (2018–2019), the number of commercial PSCs operating in Pakistan decreased to 87 (Figs. 3.1 and 3.2), representing a 51% decline since 2016–2017. Despite the reduction in the number of SOEs, there has been no notable decline in the number of public sector employees, which

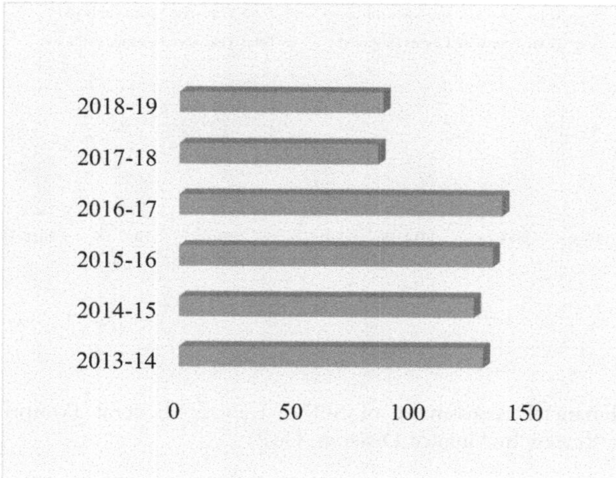

Fig. 3.1 Number of Commercial SOEs. (*Source*: Federal Footprint: SOEs Performance Review by Finance Division, GoP)

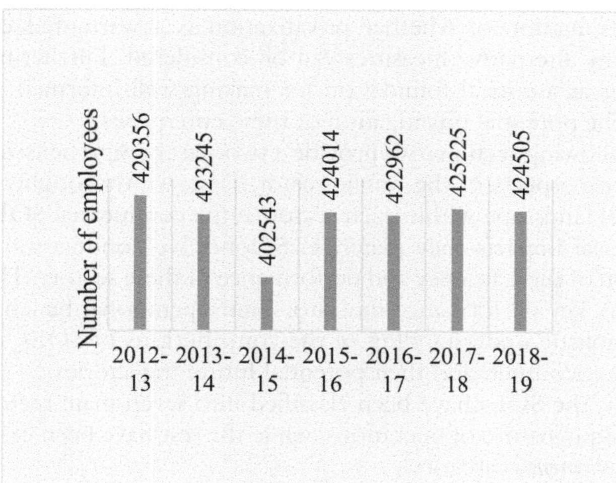

Fig. 3.2 Total Employment in SOEs. (*Source*: Federal Footprint: SOEs Performance Review by Finance Division, GoP)

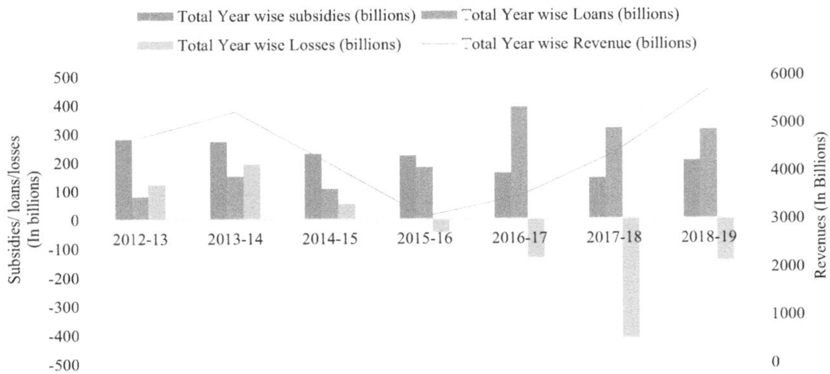

Fig. 3.3 Financial Assessment of SOEs. (*Source*: Federal Footprint: SOEs Performance Review by Finance Division, GoP)

remains a potential reason for the economic burden caused by these inefficient SOEs.

In light of the facts discussed above, it is an inevitable need of a detailed assessment of the financial landscape of sector-wise commercial SOEs, and examining the fiscal implications they impose. The objective is to seek an informed evaluation of whether privatization is a warranted course of action or any alternative measures can be considered. Furthermore, this study serves as a critical foundation for making well-informed decisions regarding the potential privatization of these enterprises.

In the following sections, we provide a two-part comprehensive analysis of the diverse aspects of the public sector. First, we thoroughly evaluate the financial landscape within each sector of the commercial SOEs, along with the fiscal impacts they generate. Second, we conduct an in-depth examination of the efficiency and performance of these sectors. This analysis considers key performance indicators and operational benchmarks to provide a holistic understanding of the contributions of SOEs, the challenges they encounter, and their potential future trajectories.

Presently, the SOEs have been classified into seven main sectors based on their unique nature of operations, while the rest have been categorized under *miscellaneous* category.

1. Financial Sector
2. Industrial and Engineering

- Manufacturing, Mining, and Engineering
- Industrial Estate Development

3. Infrastructure, Transport, and ITC
4. Power and Energy
5. Oil and Gas
6. Trading and Marketing
7. Miscellaneous
    - Services sector
    - Promotional and Advocacy

1. **Financial Sector**

The financial sector in Pakistan includes banks, non-bank financial institutions (NBFIs), development finance institutions (DFIs), and insurance companies. It is considered to be one of the most stable sectors in terms of net cash flows and other important indicators such as revenue and net profits. In 2018, out of a total of 87 SOEs, 18 SOEs was operating in the financial sector, while in 2013–2014, they were 33 in numbers as shown in Fig. 3.4. As far as the employment status of the financial sector is concerned, it has experienced a 13% decline in employment since 2013 (Fig. 3.5), employing a total of 29,000 employees.

As far the revenue assessment is concerned, Fig. 3.5 shows that the financial sector has witnessed a significant increase in revenues from Rs.

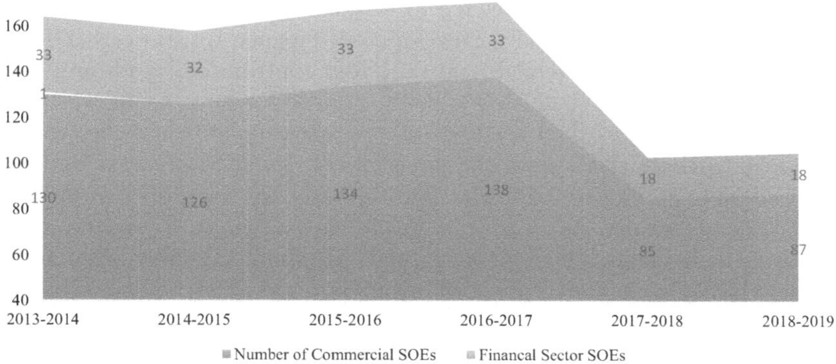

Fig. 3.4 Number of Commercial SOEs in the Financial Sector. (*Source*: Federal Footprint: SOEs Performance Review by Finance Division, GoP)

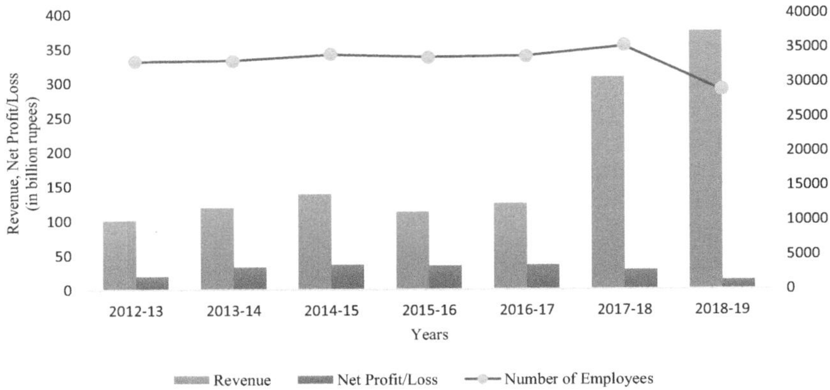

Fig. 3.5 Financial Assessment of SOEs in Financial Sector. (*Source*: Federal Footprint: SOEs Performance Review by Finance Division, GoP)

119 billion in 2013 to Rs. 374 billion in 2019. This indicates a more than 200% increase in net revenues. The National Strategic Financial Inclusion Strategy played a significant role in this increase, as it helped to enhance access to the banking system of the country, leading to more loan disbursements in these years. A decline in net profits can be observed from 28 billion rupees in 2018 to 13 billion rupees in 2019. Despite that it remained positive throughout the years under study. However, Pakistan's banking sector faced significant challenges following the nationalization of banks in 1974. Political interference in day-to-day operations, particularly in hiring and lending decisions, led to financial indiscipline and a decline in service quality. Additionally, Development Finance Institutions (DFIs) and Nationalized Commercial Banks (NCBs) contributed significantly to the accumulation of bad debts, with non-performing loans (NPLs) accounting for approximately 90% of the banking industry's total. In response to these challenges, the government opted to privatize several banks despite being profitable and not imposing any fiscal burden on the government treasury. As a result, it was initially decided to privatize two relatively small banks, Allied Bank Limited (ABL) and Muslim Commercial Bank (MCB), in the initial phase of privatization in 1991.

2. **Industrial and Engineering Sector**

This sector is diverse and encompasses a wide range of industries and businesses involved in manufacturing, construction, and engineering activities, contributing significantly to the country's economy and industrial growth. While analyzing the Industrial and Engineering sector, it can be seen that in 2014, there were a total of 21 SOEs operating in this sector (Fig. 3.6) which declined to 20 in 2017. Furthermore, after 2017, the Industrial and Engineering sector was split into two categories: "Manufacturing, Mining & Engineering," and "Industrial Estate Development."

This sector has struggled financially in recent years, with several SOEs, including Pakistan Steel Mills, contributing to its poor performance. The revenues decreased significantly from around 48 billion rupees in 2013 to around 20 billion rupees in 2017, representing a decrease of approximately 58%. Moreover, the sector consistently incurred losses, however, there is a decrease in losses from 25 billion rupees in 2013 to around 13 billion rupees in 2017. The amount of domestic and foreign loans dispersed to the sector also increased from 3 billion to 4.3 billion rupees, likely due to its poor financial performance. It received the highest amount of debt in 2015 after which a decline can be observed (Fig. 3.7).

Similarly, a highest number of employees (22827) could be observed in 2014–2015, after which it experienced a decline (Fig. 3.8).

3. **The Industrial Estate Development Sector**

Industrial Estate Development became a separate category after the re-categorization of Industrial and Engineering sector since 2018. Out of a total of 85 SOEs in 2018 and 2019, only four operate in Industrial Estate

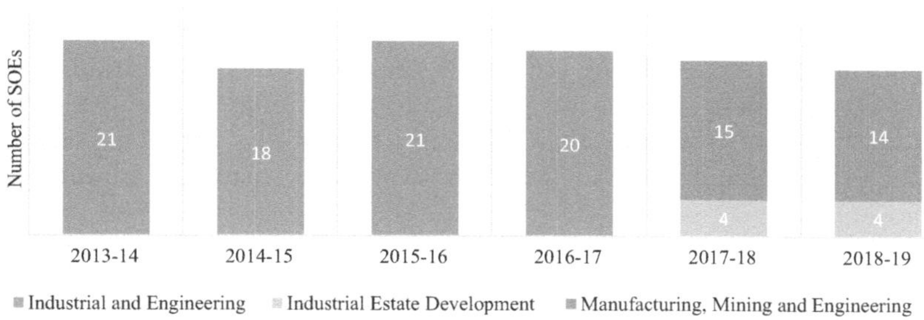

Fig. 3.6 Number of SOEs in Industrial and Engineering Sector

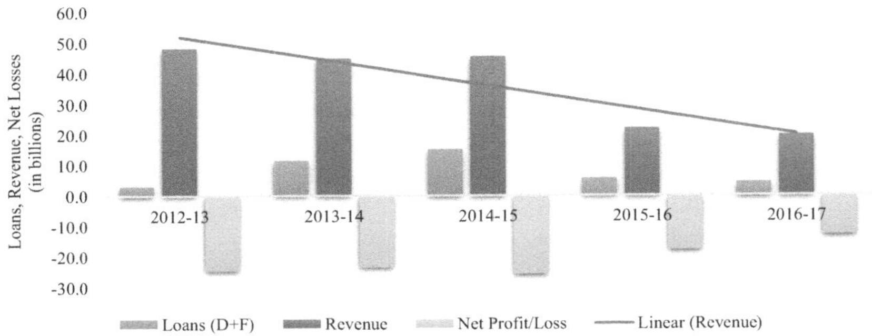

Fig. 3.7 Financial Status of Industrial and Engineering Sector

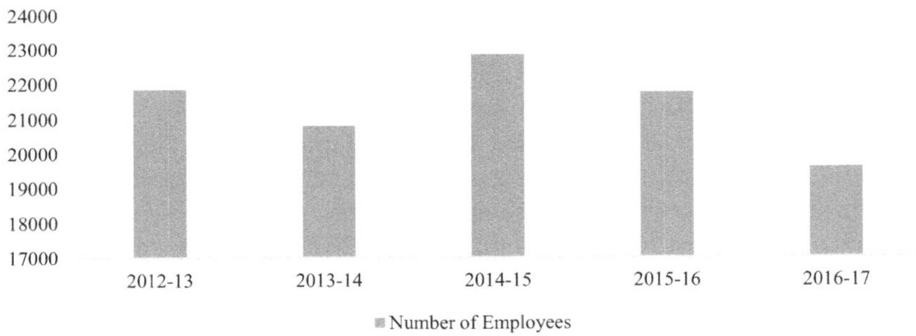

Fig. 3.8 Number of Employees in Industrial and Engineering Sector. (*Source*: Federal Footprint: SOEs Performance Review by Finance Division, GoP)

Development (see Fig. 3.6), which deals with construction, export processing, and textiles.

Despite that the initial loans of the companies in the Industrial and Engineering sector were being waived off, the newly categorized Industrial Estate Development sector has reported a total loss of more than Rs. 394 million, an increase of more than 400% in losses in one year. This sector has been struggling to manage cash flows and maintain minimum employability.

As of 2018 and 2019, the SOEs in Industrial Estate Development employed more than 1000 people, with a 6% decrease in employment since 2018 (Fig. 3.9).

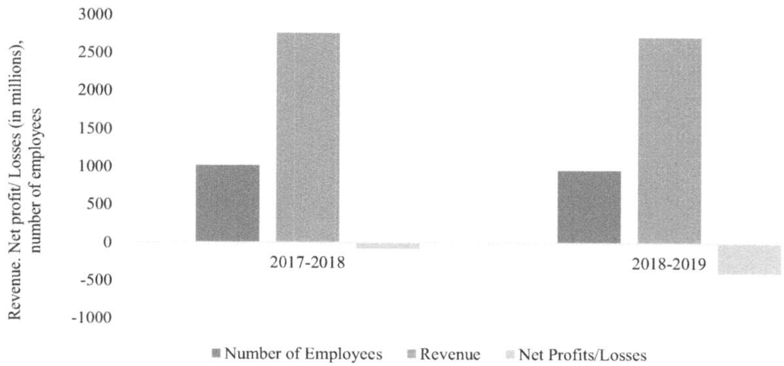

Fig. 3.9 Status of Industrial Estate Development. (*Source*: Federal Footprint: SOEs Performance Review by Finance Division, GoP)

4. **Manufacturing, Mining, and Engineering Sector**
The Manufacturing, Mining, and Engineering sector comprises of companies involved in metals and mining, engineering consultancy, and printing. In 2019, 14 SOEs operated in this sector, including industries previously categorized under Industrial and Engineering.

As far as the financial performance is concerned, the sector experienced a significant decrease in net losses, from Rs. 138 billion in 2018 to Rs. 12.9 billion in 2019. However, revenues earned by this sector remained the same (24 billion) as shown in Fig. 3.11. In 2019, 0.73 billion rupees of subsidies and 6.6 billion rupees of loans were dispersed to this sector. As of 2019, the Manufacturing and Engineering sector employed approximately 2100 people, marking an 18% decrease in employment since 2018 (shown in Fig. 3.10).

5. **Services Sector**
The Government of Pakistan provides various services in the areas of construction, telecommunications, housing, training and development, and also operates the national post office. In 2017, there were a total of 26 state-owned enterprises in the services sector. This sector was included in the miscellaneous category in 2018.

As far as the financial status is concerned, the sector has been experiencing increasing revenues on one hand and mounting losses on the other. The total revenue earned by this sector shows an increase of 35% from 43

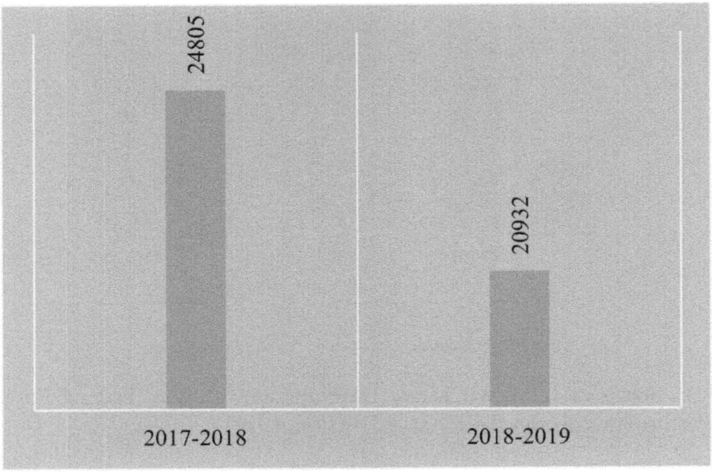

Fig. 3.10 Number of Employees. (*Source*: Federal Footprint: SOEs Performance Review by Finance Division, GoP)

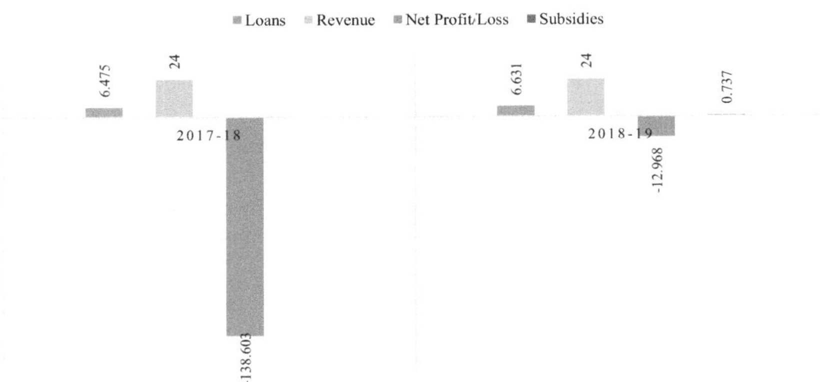

Fig. 3.11 Financial Analysis of Manufacturing, Mining, and Engineering Sector. (*Source*: Federal Footprint: SOEs Performance Review by Finance Division, GoP)

billion in 2013 to 58 billion in 2017. However, Fig. 3.12 shows that the services sector has been experiencing an increase in losses throughout the period under study from 2.9 billion in 2013 to 6.9 billion in 2017. However, the loans (domestic +foreign) disbursed to this sector decreased from 205 million to 34 million rupees during the same period. It is noteworthy that Pakistan Post Office, which operates under this sector, has been the largest source of losses (Fig. 3.13).

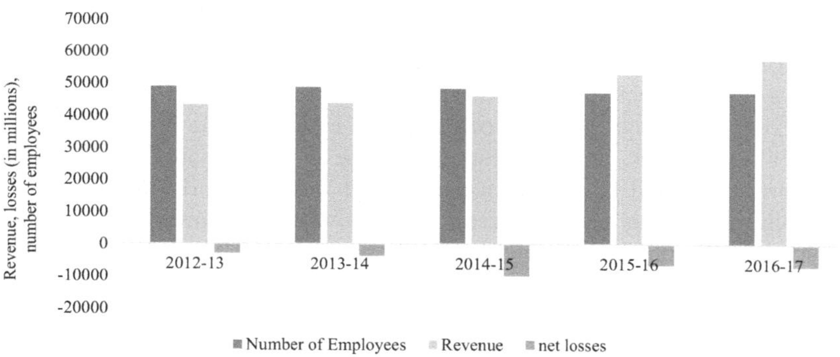

Fig. 3.12 Financial and Employment Status of Services Sector. (*Source*: Federal Footprint: SOEs Performance Review by Finance Division, GoP)

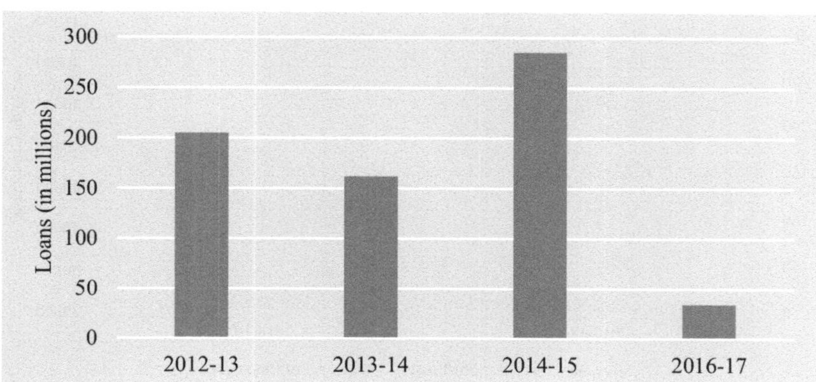

Fig. 3.13 Loans (Domestic + Foreign) in Services Sector. (*Source*: Federal Footprint: SOEs Performance Review by Finance Division, GoP)

As far as the employability in this sector is concerned, it employed more than 4700 people in 2017, representing a 2% decline in employment since 2013.

6. **Oil and Gas Sector**

The Oil and Gas sector is of significant importance for the economy with a total of eight SOEs currently operating within this industry. Prior to 2017, the Oil and Gas sector was part of the Power and Energy sector, however, in 2018 it was categorized as a separate category due to its importance for the economy.

According to data from 2018 and 2019, the Oil and Gas sector experienced a notable increase in both revenues and net profits. In 2019, the sector recorded a net revenue of Rs. 2908 billion, while in 2018 it was 2303 billion rupees, representing an increase of more than 26%. In addition, profits earned by this sector increased from around 198 billion to 242 billion over this period. Despite this growth, the number of employees in the Oil and Gas sector has seen a significant decline, with around more than 40,000 individuals employed in 2019. It is worth noting that the Oil and Gas sector did not receive any loans or subsidies during 2018 and 2019 (Fig. 3.14).

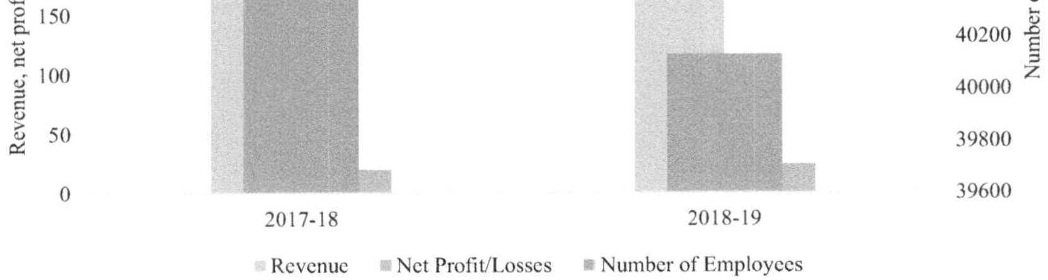

Fig. 3.14 Financial and Employment Status of Oil and Gas Sector. (*Source*: Federal Footprint: SOEs Performance Review by Finance Division, GoP)

7. **Power Sector**

The power sector is also considered as the backbone of any economy, as it is involved in power generation, distribution, and transmission activities. However, in recent years, the power and energy sector has seen a decline in revenues and an increase in losses, despite receiving government support through subsidies and loans. In 2019, the power and energy sector had a total of 21 SOEs operating within it.

As far as the revenues are concerned, the sector has witnessed a significant decline from 4198 billion in 2013 to 1888 billion in 2019 which depicts a 55% decline in revenues (shown in Fig. 3.15).

As far as the net profitability is concerned, the power sector has initially been profitable, however, it incurred huge losses in 2017–2018. However, it is among one of the few sectors availing continuous subsidies and loans. This sector has received over 43 billion in grants in 2016, and 749 billion rupees in loans between 2013 and 2019, resulting in a debt to revenue ratio of 3.5% since 2013. Figure 3.15 demonstrates the sector's dependency on loans and subsidies.

Despite the government's support, the power and energy sector's financial performance has been deteriorating. The sector's decline in revenue and increasing losses have far-reaching consequences, given its importance to the economy. Therefore, there is a need to reassess the sector's financial management and to develop a sustainable financing model to ensure its long-term viability (Fig. 3.16).

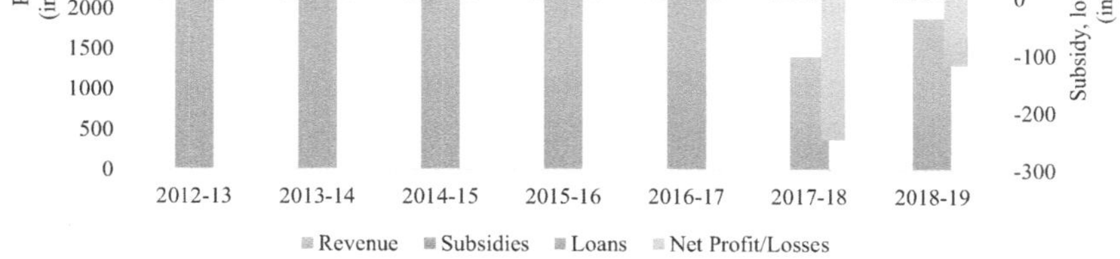

Fig. 3.15 Financial Assessment of Power Sector. (*Source*: Federal Footprint: SOEs Performance Review by Finance Division, GoP)

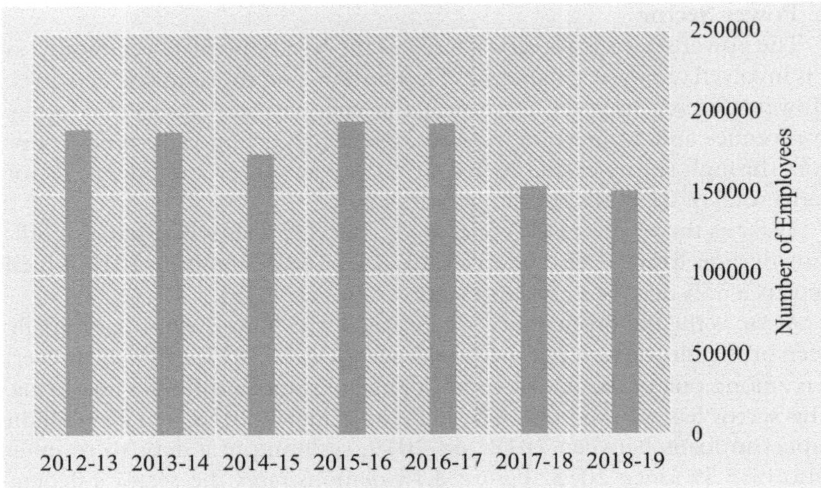

Fig. 3.16 Employment in Power Sector. (*Source*: Federal Footprint: SOEs Performance Review by Finance Division, GoP)

As of 2019, this sector employed around 150,000 people. However, the sector has also seen a significant decline of 26% in employment since 2013.

Furthermore, due to its reliance on external funding, there is a need for the sector to diversify its funding sources and explore more sustainable financial models. Additionally, the decline in employment underscores the need for the sector to prioritize job creation initiatives and invest in human resource development to ensure a skilled workforce in the future.

8. **Infrastructure and Transportation Sector**

The Infrastructure and Transportation sector includes companies related to ports, shipping, roads, highways, aviation, and communication. Currently, there are a total of 12 SOEs operating in this sector.

Financial analysis of this sector reveals an increasing trend both in revenues and losses (Fig. 3.17). The total revenue earned by this sector increased from 187 billion to 429 billion during 2013–2019. Similarly, the net losses also increased from 98 billion to 267 billion rupees which is a 172% increase since 2013 (as shown in Fig. 3.17).

Moreover, Fig. 3.18 shows that since 2016, the sector has also been receiving subsidies in addition to loans, while earlier it did not. A total of

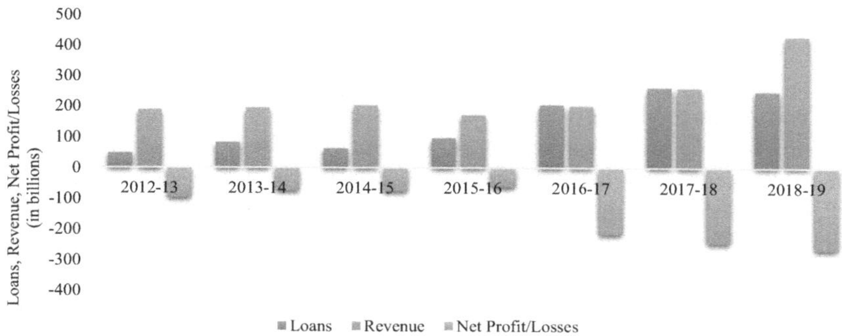

Fig. 3.17 Financial Status of Transport, Infrastructure, and ITC sector

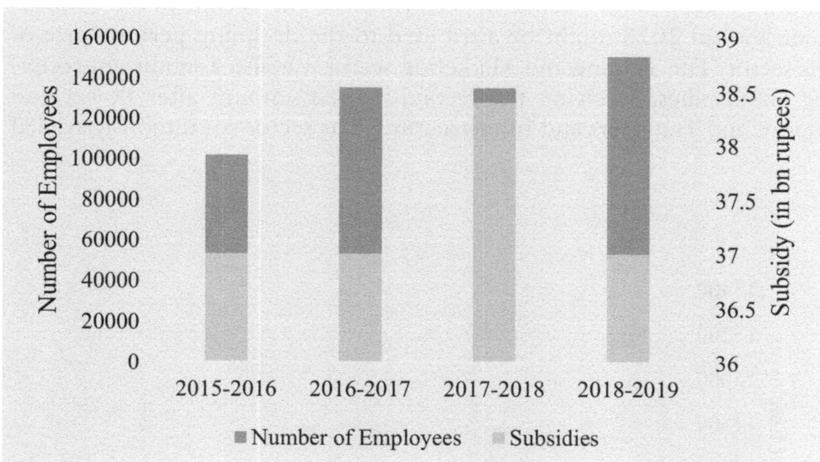

Fig. 3.18 Subsidy and Employability in Transport, Infrastructure, and ITC

149 billion rupees were transferred to the sector in the form of subsidies between 2016 and 2019. Moreover, between 2013 and 2015, a total of Rs. 103 billion was disbursed in the form of grants to the sector, accounting for approximately 18% of its net revenues in those years. Similarly, the total amount of loans disbursed to this sector between 2013 and 2019 mounted to Rs. 999 billion. Given the sector's significant reliance on loans and subsidies, it is crucial to reevaluate its financial management and develop sustainable financing models to ensure its long-term viability.

As of 2019, the sector employs more than 150,000 individuals, including it among the top SOEs in terms of employment.

9. **Trading and Marketing Sector**

The Trading and Marketing sector encompasses SOEs involved in wholesale, retail, and marketing activities. As of 2019, the sector had only four operating SOEs, including Utility Stores Corporation Private Limited. In 2019, the sector employed less than 15,000 people, indicating a 5% decline in employment since 2017 (Fig. 3.19).

The financial data for the sector from 2014 to 2018 shows a decline in performance. While the sector was profitable in the early years, it started to incur losses since 2017. The decrease in revenue from approximately 130 billion rupees in 2013 to 63 billion rupees in 2019 was the main contributing factor to the decline in performance. The decline in the employment level in 2018 might be attributed to the declining performance of this sector. The Trading and Marketing sector was also a significant recipient of subsidies, receiving the second-highest amount after Power and Energy, and Transport and Infrastructure. The sector continuously availed

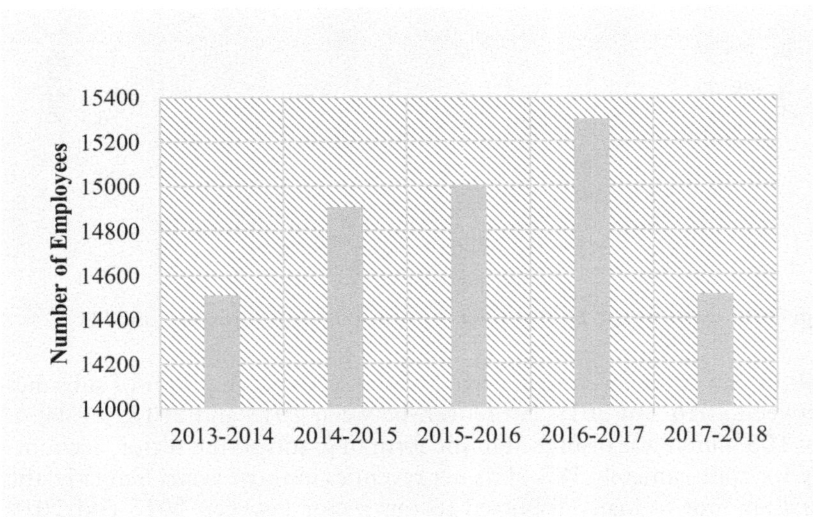

Fig. 3.19 Employment in Trading and Marketing Sector. (*Source*: Federal Footprint: SOEs Performance Review by Finance Division, GoP)

subsidies, amounting to Rs. 206 billion between 2013 and 2019. This amount represented 35% as a share of the sector's total revenue earned during the same period. The unsatisfactory performance of the Trading and Marketing sector despite its potential for growth is a matter of great concern. The sector's reliance on subsidies and losses incurred over the years indicates a need for restructuring and improvement in its operations (Fig. 3.20).

10. **Promotional and Advocacy Sector**

The SOEs in the Promotional and Advocacy sector faced significant challenges in recent years. In 2017, a total number of 46 SOEs operated in this sector, and the majority (41) were non-commercial organizations, including various foundations working on humanitarian basis. The remaining five SOEs were commercial.

Unfortunately, the available data indicates that in 2017, the sector recorded a staggering loss of over 29 billion rupees. However, the sector's total revenue increased by 34% from 109 billion in 2013 to 16.5 billion in 2017 (Fig. 3.21).

As of 2017, the Promotional and Advocacy sector provided employment to around 9200 employees and witnessed a 69% increase in employment since 2013. Due to huge losses, however, the sector also witnessed a decrease of 11% in employment since 2016.

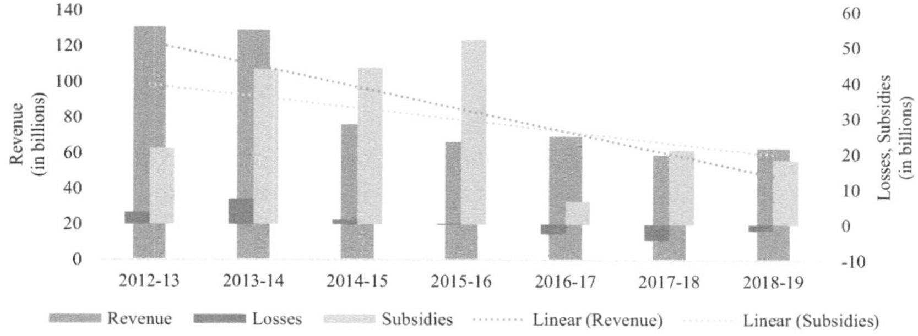

Fig. 3.20 Financial Analysis of Trading and Marketing Sector. (*Source*: Federal Footprint: SOEs Performance Review by Finance Division, GoP)

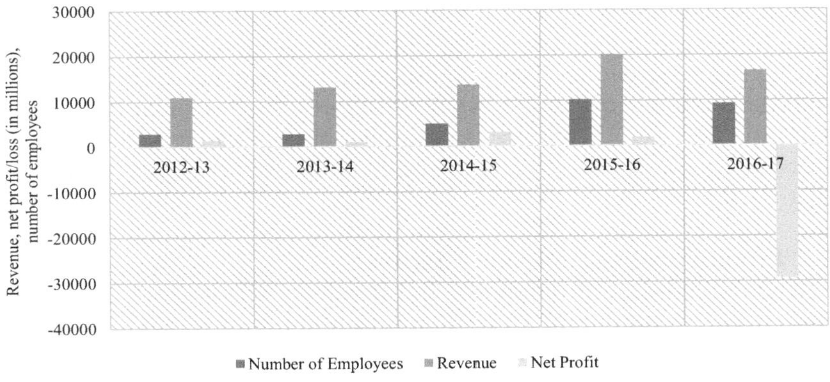

Fig. 3.21 Financial Status of Promotional and Advocacy. (*Source*: Federal Footprint: SOEs Performance Review by Finance Division, GoP)

11. **Miscellaneous**

The *Miscellaneous* category comprises of six companies, including the Pakistan Broadcasting Corporation (PTC), Pakistan Television Corporation Limited (PTVC), and Pakistan Tourism Development Corporation (PTDC).

From 2018 to 2019, the firms in the *Miscellaneous category* experienced an increase in revenues (from 15.5 billion to 17.3 billion) and a decrease in net losses (from 1.7 billion to 0.05 billion) as shown in Fig. 3.22. In 2019, the sector recorded an 11% increase in revenues compared to 2018, and net losses decreased by 36%. The YoY analysis further suggests that the sector's productive capacity has not only increased but has also grown at a rapid pace. Additionally, there has been a 56% decrease in loans, indicating the potential for growth in the sector.

It is worth noting that the *miscellaneous* category initially comprised 72 companies operating in both the Services, and Promotional and Advocacy sectors, but the number was reduced to six during the re-categorization process. Despite this reduction, this sector employed around 8000 people as of 2019. However, there has been a significant decrease in employment as well since 2018.

Overall, firms in the *Miscellaneous* category have the potential for growth without subsidies and loans, as demonstrated by the significant increase in revenues and decrease in net losses (Fig. 3.23).

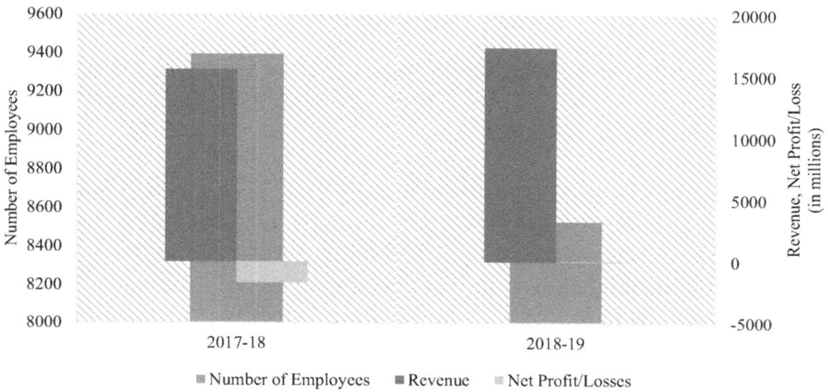

Fig. 3.22 Financial Assessment of SOEs in Miscellaneous Category. (*Source*: Federal Footprint: SOEs Performance Review by Finance Division, GoP)

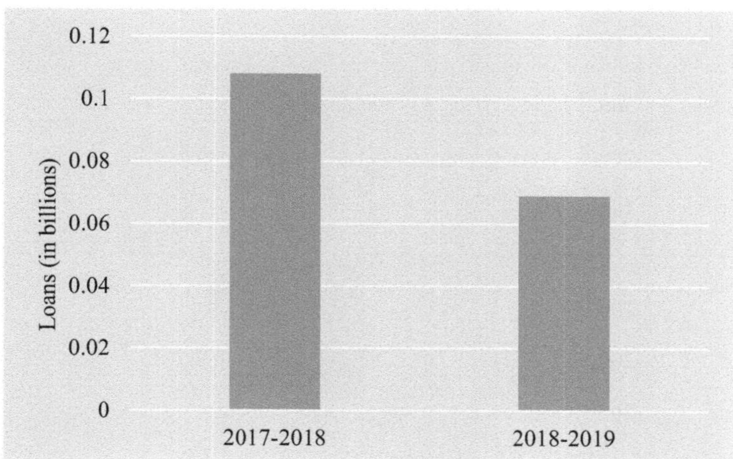

Fig. 3.23 Loans Disbursed to SOEs in Miscellaneous Category

Key Take-aways

Based on our analysis of financial position of sector-wise SOEs in terms of revenue, net profit/losses, we come to the following conclusions (Figs. 3.24 and 3.25, Table 3.1):

- Among all the sectors, *Infrastructure, Transport, & ITC* ranked at the highest in making the largest amount of losses in 2018–2019, with the cumulative losses of 512 billion during 2013–2019.
- It is followed by Power and Energy, being of high relevance for the economy, making losses of 117 billion rupees, with the cumulative losses amounting to 364 billion rupees.
- Contrary to that both these sectors incur the largest amount of fiscal burden in the form of subsidies and loans.
- Power and Energy takes the lead in securing 147 billion rupees of subsidies in 2018–2019 followed by Infrastructure, Transport, & ITC, and Trading and Marketing.

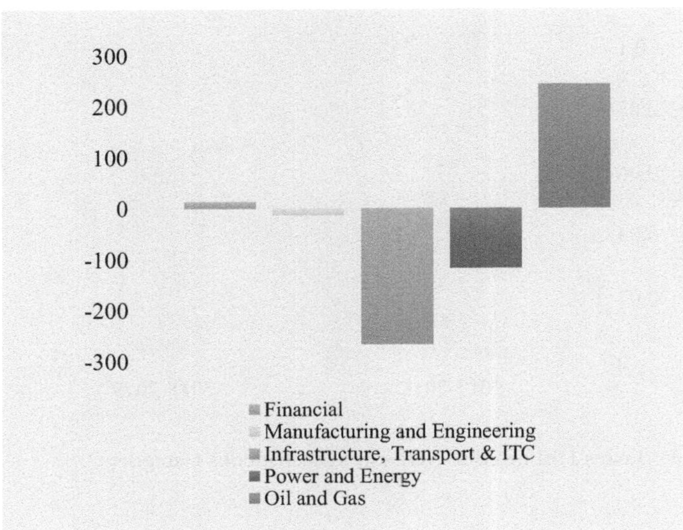

Fig. 3.24 Net Profit/Losses in 2018–2019. (*Source*: Federal Footprint: SOEs Performance Review by Finance Division, GoP)

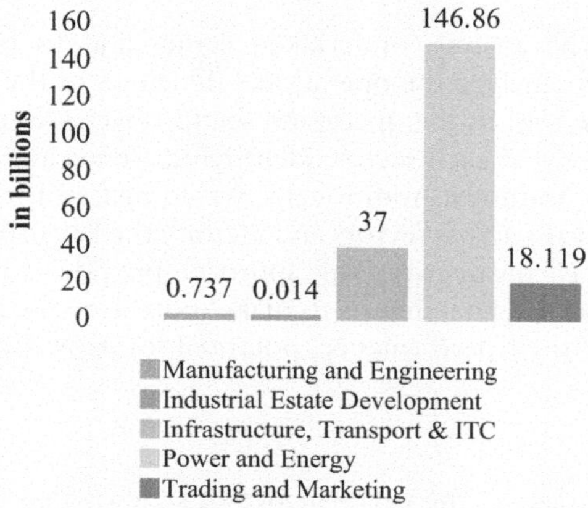

Fig. 3.25 Sector-wise Allocation of Subsidies, 2018–2019. (*Source*: Federal Footprint: SOEs Performance Review by Finance Division, GoP)

Table 3.1 Fiscal burden of SOEs, 2019

Variables	*Industrial estate development*	*Manufacturing & Engineering*	*Infrastructure, Transport & ITC*	*Power*	*Misc.*	*Oil & Gas*	*Trading & Marketing*
Subsidies	0.014	0.74	37	147	–	–	18
Loans	–	6.63	248	56	0.06	0.02	0
Liabilities	7	289	3254	6852	53	1354	235
Total (in billion)	7	297	3539	7055	53	1354	271

- On the other hand, Oil and Gas has been a highly profitable sector in 2018–2019, without receiving any subsidies from the government.
- The Infrastructure, Transport, and ITC, and Power sectors are also putting a huge financial and fiscal burden on the government, amounting to 3539 and 7055 billion PKR, respectively. The poor rate of return (RoR) scenario has further declined the investment opportunities for these sectors.

Sectoral Analysis of Performance and Efficiency of SOEs

To complement the analysis undertaken earlier and to have a deeper insight, we need to analyze the operational dynamics of the public sector as well. To achieve this, in the upcoming sections we assessed the performance and efficiency of each sector, identifying trends and patterns that are specific to that industry. Additionally, we compared the performance and efficiency of SOEs across sectors and identify the key drivers of success and failure within each category. This approach provides a more granular view of the SOE sector, enabling us to make more accurate and insightful conclusions about their performance, potential for growth, and areas for improvement.

(a) **Performance**

As a standard practice, the performance of state-owned sectors can be assessed through the analysis of their sales, assets, rate of return (ROR), and net profit/sale ratio. Recent data from various sources in 2019 shows that 87 commercial SOEs are currently operational, and their performance varies in the market. The net profit/sale ratio is a key metric used to assess the performance of these firms. As a general rule of thumb, 5% is the lower margin and 10% is a relatively healthier margin indicating a higher performance of the firms. Whereas, negative profit/sale ratio indicates lower performance of the firm which also shows a firm's lower control over its expenses. According to this rule of thumb, all the sectors are performing poorly. While if we judge the performance of the sectors just on the basis of positive values, then the data in Table 3.2 depicts that except for Oil and Gas, Financial sector, and firms in the miscellaneous sector, all the other sectors are performing low in terms of *rate of return (ROR)* and *profit-sale ratio*. Let us discuss the performance of each sector one by one.

The Oil and Gas sector is considered to be the backbone of the economy which is involved in all types of activities related to exploration, refining, marketing, and distribution of oil and gas. It has been the highest sales producing sector in 2019 having a revenue generation of around 2909 billion rupees. Despite that the RoR (net profits to asset ratio) in this sector has been only 0.09. Though the RoR is positive and higher as compared to other sectors yet according to the global standards, it is not performing at par.

Table 3.2 Performance of SOEs (2018–2019)

Variables	*Trading & Marketing*	*Manufacturing, Mining & Engineering*	*Infrastructure, Transport, & ITC*	*Power*	*Industrial Estate Development*	*Misc.*	*Oil & Gas*	*Financial Sector*
Sales (Rs. billion)	62.8	24	429	1888	2.7	17.3	2909	374
Assets (Rs. billion)	297.5	496.7	5348	7846	17.3	28.7	2646	4904
Net-profits/ Sales Ratio	−0.03	−0.5	−0.62	−0.06	−0.14	0.002	0.08	0.04
Rate of Return	−0.006	-0.03	−0.05	−0.01	−0.02	0.002	0.09	0.003

Source: Authors' calculations based on data from Federal Footprint: SOEs Performance Review by Finance Division, GoP

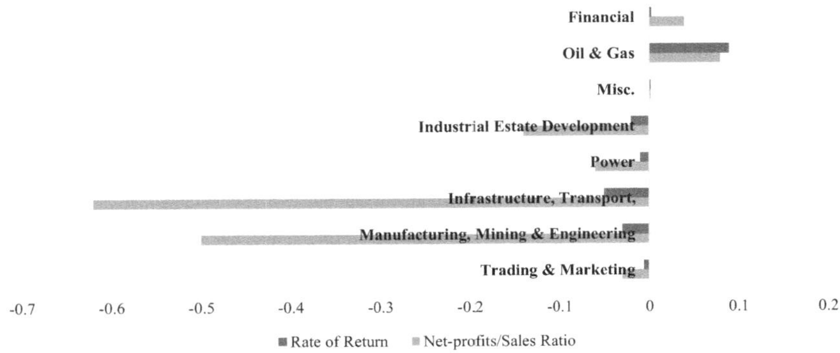

Fig. 3.26 Performance of SOEs (2018–2019). (*Source*: Authors' calculations based on data from Federal Footprint: SOEs Performance Review by Finance Division, GoP)

The performance of the sectors in the government ownership can also be judged from Fig. 3.26.

After oil and gas comes another key sector of the economy which is the Power sector with a total sale of 1888 billion PKR in 2019. Power sector is engaged in all activities including generation, distribution, transmission, and management of power in the country. Despite having a key position in the running of the economy, the performance measures show a gloomy picture when it comes to the rate of return and marginal profits. Both the values are negative showing a situation of net loss in this sector.

Financial sector exhibits a relatively better performance with an increase of 22% in its net income in 2019. It had a rate of return (RoR) of 0.003 in 2019 which is not an indication of high profitability or gain. However, a positive RoR is the indication of gain on investment, suggesting a positive signal for more private investment too. When it comes to understanding the financial segmentation of the country, Pakistan is one of the few countries in the world that has not seen the success of its Development Finance Institutions (DFIs). Farouqi (2015) while highlighting the causes of failures of DFIs in Pakistan in comparison to the success of the same in Korea and China states that the main aim of DFIs is to establish a strong industrial base for performing massive contributions to the economy; however, the import outlook of the country has always been consumerism. DFIs have been used to pay for the trade deficits and the same can be seen in the case of Bankers Equity Limited. Therefore, instead of using the micro-long-term finances for developing heavy industrial zones in the country, the same has been used majorly to import the goods from other countries thereby increasing the cost of production for the same and also increasing the completion time for the projects.

Unfortunately, the rest of the sectors have performed extremely poorly in terms of RoR. They have shown major performance issues. For example, the Infrastructure and Transport sector is the third largest sector when it comes to assets holding, that is, 5341 billion PKR, however, the sector only recorded a sale of 427 billion PKR in 2019. Such a small number shows that the marginal productivity of the sector has been torn down.

(b) **Efficiency**

Though performance is an indicator of efficiency, but when it comes to the efficiency of the sectors in real terms, it has to be measured through sales to employment ratio. Sales to employment shows per capita productivity which leads to the path toward optimization. Also, sales to employment ratio allows us to study the marginal productivity of the sector in terms of the labor dynamics. Goher (2012) in her study pointed out the fact that the highest loss-making enterprise owned by the government has the highest number of employees and pensioners, therefore, they usually suffer major losses. However, it is not the number of employees but their productivity through which the performance of a sector can be judged.

Looking at the sector-wise efficiency scenario in Table 3.3, we can see that the Oil and Gas sector has the most optimal share in the efficiency paradigm. In 2021, the total market was shared by 18 companies and out of which 8 were owned by the state. Pakistan State Oil (PSO) is the state benchmark in this regard. It held more than 45% of the total market capital and has seen an increase of 23% in its shareholders' equity for the year 2021. It also contributed to its profit during the same year, making it the most efficient sector of all with the ratio of 72.51.

After the oil and gas sector comes the *power* sector having an efficiency score of 12.5 in 2018–2019 though this sector has been making losses since 2017–2018. These losses have mainly been due to the distribution companies and the circular debt they have accumulated over the years.

Among all the remaining sectors, Manufacturing and Engineering has shown the least efficiency in the recent years not just because of high level of employment but also due to low level of revenues, both causing a reduction in the marginal productivity of these sectors.

Table 3.3 Efficiency of SOEs

Sales/Employment ratio	*Industrial Estate Development*	*Manufacturing & Engineering*	*Infrastructure, Transport & ITC*	*Power*	*Misc.*	*Oil & Gas*	*Trading & Marketing*
2018–2019	2.8	1.13	2.8	12.5	2.0	72.5	4.3
2017–2018	2.7	0.96	1.9	9.19	1.6	56.1	3.8
2016–2017	2.6	1.0	1.47	15.5	1.6	54.5	4.6

Source: Authors' calculations based on data from Federal Footprint: SOEs Performance Review by Finance Division, GoP

Such low levels of efficiency indicate that the sectors need to revamp their priorities and align them with the changing dynamics of neo-administrative regimes. In the past, most of the SOEs which were privatized were from the construction sector, and out of those, most of them have closed their operations. They could not survive in a highly competitive market and required transitional period for market adjustment. However, due to inefficient productive capacities, most of the previously privatized SOEs could not sustain market pressures.

Concluding Remarks

After the examination of the financial health and fiscal burden of SOEs, it is concluded that the overall picture revealed by the data and analysis is concerning, indicating that the situation demands attention. These circumstances call for exploring potential solutions to address the issues with SOEs. Two main avenues emerge as potential solutions, each with its own set of implications.

The first approach involves a comprehensive overhaul of the way SOEs are managed, which would require significant structural reforms and a reimagining of their role within the public framework. While this option holds promise in theory, it is important to acknowledge the practical challenges associated with such a massive undertaking. Implementing such a reform could require substantial time, resources, and coordination across various levels of governance. Therefore, the first approach may not be a quick fix and may require a long-term commitment from the government and other stakeholders. However, if successfully implemented, this approach could lead to a more efficient and effective management of SOEs, resulting in better financial health and economic impact.

The second option is to privatize the SOEs, which means transferring ownership or management control to private sector experts who have experience in optimizing performance and efficiency. This option is considered more pragmatic because it allows the government to leverage the power of market dynamics and tap into the expertise of those who excel in managing and growing businesses. By privatizing the SOEs, the government can potentially improve their performance and efficiency, which could lead to economic growth. This option also has the potential to alleviate the fiscal burden on the government, as the private sector experts may be able to run the SOEs more efficiently and profitably.

However, there are also potential drawbacks to privatization, such as the loss of government control over the SOEs and the potential for private sector interests to conflict with the public interest. Therefore, the government must consider both immediate and long-term consequences of their actions on the economy. Striking a balance between these options requires careful evaluation and a clear understanding of the broader impact on sectors, industries, and the workforce. This means that the policymakers must take into account the impact of their actions on different segments of the economy and the people who work in those areas.

The road ahead may be intricate, which means that the decision-making process may be complex and difficult. However, the central goal remains clear—to fortify the economy, drive sustainable growth, and secure a prosperous future for all stakeholders including workers, businesses, and citizens.

Reference

Finance Division, G. o. (n.d.). *Federal footprint: State-owned entitiesperformance overview*. Implementation and Economic Reforms Unit.

PART II

Exploratory and Empirical Assessments of Privatization

CHAPTER 4

Exploratory Analysis of Privatization

Abstract While privatization has led to improved rates of return on assets, but in general, non-profitability persisted, raising concerns about its effectiveness in enhancing efficiency, particularly in under-developed nations like Pakistan. Therefore, Chap. 4 provides an exploratory analysis of privatization in Pakistan, focusing on the performance, efficiency, competitiveness, and fiscal burden of SOEs before and after privatization. This chapter also evaluates various indicators such as rate of returns, net profit-to-asset ratio, and concentration ratios to assess the impact of privatization. Marginal gains in competitiveness post-privatization were observed, but market power still existed for the privatized firms. The chapter also discusses the fiscal impact and notes partial relief following privatization. Overall, it emphasizes the need for a clear approach to address the issues faced by SOEs, while emphasizing that further empirical analysis is required due to complexities surrounding privatization efforts.

Keywords Privatization program • Deregulation • Disinvestment • Economic reforms • Efficiency

Despite successful attempts toward privatization in the past, the presence of government intervention is still substantial in public sector enterprises in Pakistan. However, the current financial outlook of these entities is not

G. Samad, N. Faraz, *The Face of Privatization in Pakistan*,
https://doi.org/10.1007/978-981-97-8385-4_4

much optimistic. Therefore, it was proposed in the preceding chapter that this situation demands either a comprehensive structural reform or a shift toward privatization. Furthermore, it was also pointed out that though structural reform is theoretically promising, it is not a straightforward solution due to its complexities. Implementing structural reform requires a significant investment of time and resources, which may not be feasible in the current situation of our country, and its feasibility will remain questionable. Consequently, a shift in strategy is recommended, where the government's role has to transform from an operator to that of a facilitator, empowering the private sector to assume the mantle of business operations.

This idea aligns with the historical context as well where the support for privatization manifested through strategic measures aimed at transferring ownership and control of public assets and services to private entities since 1990.

Though the overall pace of privatization in Pakistan has been slow due to challenges such as legal hurdles, political opposition, and resistance from labor unions. Despite that, the Privatization Commission has successfully privatized or semi-privatized a total of 178 public sector corporations (PSCs), generating 649,114 million rupees ($11 billion) in revenue for the government from 1991 to 2021. The largest amount of privatization proceeds came from the capital market, followed by the telecommunication sector (depicted in Fig. 4.1).

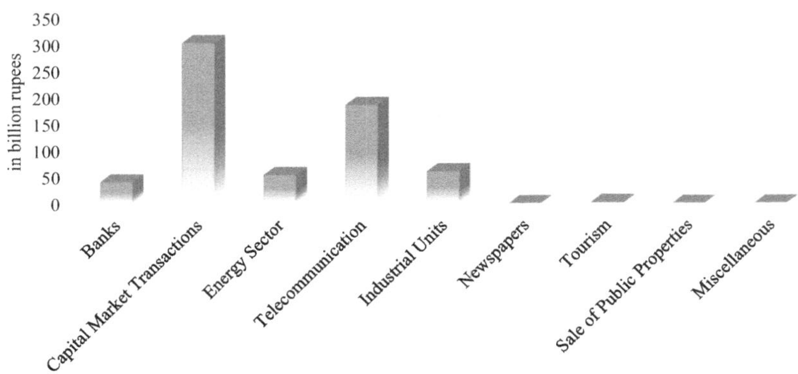

Fig. 4.1 Sector-wise Privatization Proceeds (billion PKR). (*Source*: Privatization Commission of Pakistan, 2023)

In continuation of the previous attempts, and as part of the IMF's Extended Fund Facility 2019–2022, the Finance Division with the collaboration of donor agencies conducted a review in late 2019 of the portfolios of 84 commercial SOEs in order to assess their impact on government finances and their effectiveness in delivering services. The decision regarding retention, deregulation, or liquidation of these SOEs had to be taken in light of this review.

The review excluded non-commercial SOEs and regulatory bodies like PEMRA and PTA. Of the 84 commercial SOEs, 25 were deemed financially viable in 2018–2019 based on their assets, net profits/losses, and return on assets, while 24 were selected for privatization, and 10 were considered for deregulation. The remaining SOEs, such as ZTBL, National Investment Trust, PTDC, and Utility Store Corporation, were identified as potential candidates for privatization in the future, subject to careful evaluation of the relevant variables. These companies included both loss-making and profit-making entities, with the majority of the latter from the financial sector, without subsidies or significant public loans.

While privatization has been proposed as a solution to the fiscal mismanagement and inefficiency of SOEs, however, in light of the previous attempts, there is still no guarantee whether this policy approach will be successful in Pakistan. Therefore, it is important to conduct an exploratory analysis of the various indicators of performance, efficiency, competitiveness, and fiscal position of the entities in the pre- and post-privatization periods.

To assess the performance of firms' pre- and post privatization, two indicators have been used including the rate of returns and the net profit-to-asset ratio. While to compare the efficiency of firms before and after privatization, sales to employment ratio has been used. Additionally, we have measured the competitiveness of privatized entities using concentration ratios and changes in the relative prices. Both an aggregated and disaggregated analysis have been conducted to get a thorough understanding of the actual situation.

Overall Analysis

Performance

Looking at the performance indicators in Figs. 4.2 and 4.3,[1] we can see that the performance of the SOEs after privatization got improved in terms of a higher and positive rate of return on assets (0.29 on average) compared to their pre-privatization period (which was −0.82). However, performance in terms of net profits to sales ratio does not exhibit a significant improvement. Though, it improved a little in the post-privatization period but has remained negative. This implies that the overall losses have declined but the SOE sector even after privatization has remained in a non-profitable position.

Thus, in order to reap up the fruit of privatization, mere reliance on the change of ownership of firms is not enough. The privatized firms must also reconsider their financial structure and management behavior. Moreover, the firms' management must ensure least amount of bureaucratic control in the firms, activities after privatization. Also, the firms' corporate health before privatization must also be taken into account. These aspects, if taken into account, will help in reaping up the fruit of privatization.

Fig. 4.2 Performance of Firms Pre- and Post-Privatization. (*Source*: Based on author's calculations)

[1] Statistics given in Appendix B (a).

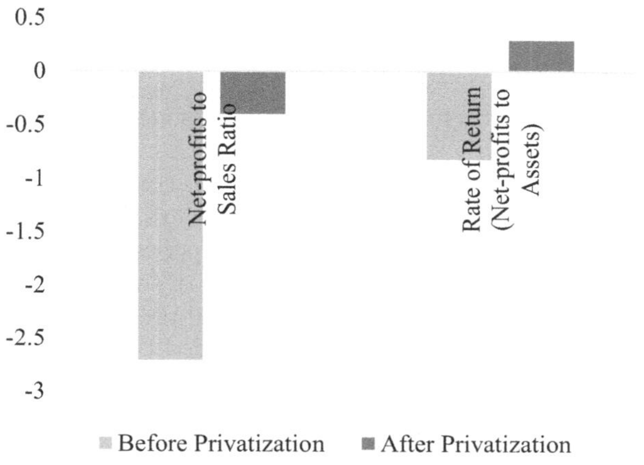

Fig. 4.3 Performance of Firms Pre- and Post-Privatization

Box 4.1 Process of Privatization

The process of privatization of the public sector enterprises in Pakistan depends on the nature of the entity to be offered for privatization. Privatization Commission board and Cabinet Committee after finalizing the mode of privatization decides on the process to be followed. The following section briefly discusses various modes of privatization mentioned in Section 25 of the PC Ordinance, 2000 and Privatization (Modes and Procedures) Rules, 2000.

First one includes the sale of assets and business which involves divesting specific assets or the entire business to private entities.

Second is the sale of shares via public auction or tender which involves offering ownership shares to the highest bidder.

Third, privatization is executed through a public offering of shares on a stock exchange which allows the general public to buy shares, potentially increasing capital and diversifying ownership.

(*continued*)

(continued)

Fourth, management or employee buyouts signifying SOE managers or employees purchasing ownership, enhancing their accountability and motivation.

Lastly, it includes lease, management, or concession contracts which include granting control or operation of the SOE to a private entity, promoting efficiency through their expertise.

Additional modes include: public offering of shares outside stock exchanges; sale of shares, assets, business, and property to individuals with pre-emptive rights, subject to specified conditions; negotiated sales; transfer of property to employee trusts of enterprises owned by the federal government under approved terms; and transferring shares via conversion of exchangeable bonds or analogous hybrid debt equity instruments, following consultation with relevant government divisions as stipulated by the Rules of Business, 1973.

After deciding on the mode of privatization, the next step is to decide on the process. The process may vary on the basis of whether it is a strategic sale or a capital market transaction. The general steps in the privatization process in both the cases are as follows:

Strategic Sales

The process of privatization in case of strategic sales involves identification of state-owned enterprises (SOEs) earmarked for privatization. Subsequently, requisite approvals are secured, including those from the Council of Common Interests (CCI) and the Cabinet Committee on Privatization (CCoP). A Financial Advisor (FA) or Valuator is engaged for the valuation process. Following this, comprehensive due diligence is conducted by both the FA and the Privatization Commission (PC). The transaction structure is then finalized, leading to the initiation of the investor solicitation phase. This involves inviting expressions of interest from potential bidders, followed by the submission of their qualifications. The pre-qualification of potential bidders ensues, followed by their in-depth due diligence. Detailed bid documents and instructions are shared, culminating in a pre-bid conference. The valuation approval is secured from the PC Board and CCoP. The public bidding process takes place, with media allowed to observe. Approval of the bidding

(*continued*)

(continued)
outcomes by the PC Board and CCoP follows. Upon selection of a successful bidder, a Letter of Intent is issued. The final stages include the execution of a Sale Agreement and the reception of proceeds from the privatization.

Capital Markets Transactions

The first few steps involved in capital market transactions are the same as that of strategic sales. However, after finalizing the structure, the process continues with the completion of regulatory prerequisites, if necessary. This is followed by the creation of a Prospectus and related promotional materials. The subsequent steps involve setting the Floor Price, conducting marketing roadshows, and initiating the Book Building process. The final price determination, known as the Strike Price, receives approval, and the allocation of shares or assets takes place. Finally, the process concludes with settlement procedures and achieving financial closure.

Efficiency

The efficiency measures predict a firm's ability to use its resources or assets effectively to produce a certain level of output. According to common perception, efficiency is a trait considered to be exhibited more by private firms and less by the SOEs. Thus, along with the performance of firms before and after privatization, it is equally important to dig into the efficiency measures as well. The efficiency measures usually include per employee indicators. Therefore, downsizing on a larger scale is the first thing which is usually done by the management of a privatized firm.

In our case, we have used *Sales to Employment Ratios* (per employee sales) as a measure to gauge the efficiency of the firms. Sales to employment ratios are supposed to increase as a result of privatization. The comparison of the pre- and post-privatization periods' efficiency ratios in Fig. 4.4 shows that on average there is an unnoticeable rise in the efficiency of the SOEs in the post-privatization period. This slight improvement in the efficiency is of great concern since privatization is advocated on the grounds that it will results in the greater efficiency of the SOEs. However, the argument of increased efficiency is stronger in the developed nations. While in under-developed nations, the outcome of

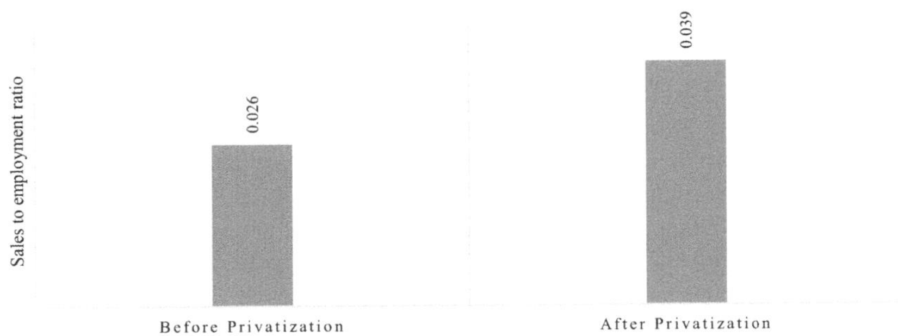

Fig. 4.4 Efficiency of Firms Pre- and Post-Privatization. (*Source*: Based on author's calculations)

privatization is mixed and complicated in nature. The reason is that there are some other factors which should be accompanied along with the privatization. These factors include institutional quality, health of capital markets, corporate rules and regulations, enforcement of copy rights, financial systems, and so on. If these factors are not in place then privatization may not lead to improved efficiency, rather it can deteriorate it further.

Competitiveness

There are few studies in case of Pakistan which have examined the competitiveness of the privatized SOEs. Most of the studies are limited to the financial sector only while those related to the non-financial sector and specifically to the manufacturing sector are non-existent.

Privatization of firms and their competitiveness in the market can be related to each other bi-directionally. Just like competitiveness in the market may lead to privatization of less competent SOEs, in the same way, privatization may lead to an increase in the competitiveness of the privatized firms. Our focus is on the latter part of the argument.

We have used two approaches to measure the competitiveness of the privatized SOEs; *concentration ratios* and the *changes in the relative prices*. The first measure—concentration ratio—has been calculated by taking the share of first four firms in each sector. Figure 4.5 illustrates that though not substantial, there are gains of competitiveness after privatization in Pakistan, judging from a decrease in the concentration ratios. The second measure—change in the relative prices—is also an indicator of

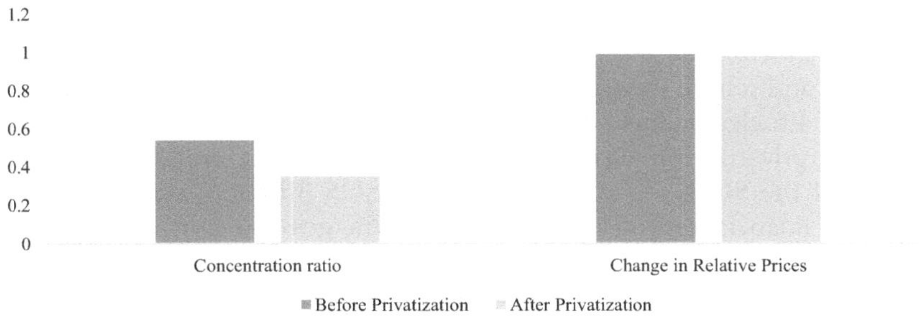

Fig. 4.5 Competitiveness of Firms before and after Privatization. (*Source*: Based on author's calculations)

competitiveness in the market. Theory suggests that competition leads to an increase in the production and a fall in the prices. Therefore, the level of market competitiveness after privatization must be reflected in the reduction of real prices of the products produced by privatized firms. Figure 4.5 depicts that the relative prices of the sectors remained nearly the same in the post-privatization period. This indicates the privatized firms did not face any kind of competition in the market and enjoyed market power even after privatization.

Fiscal Burden

The relationship channel between SOEs and the budget works bi-directionally: from SOEs to the budget in the form of taxes and dividends, and from budget to the SOEs in the form of subsidies, loans, guarantees, and grants. This transmission path implies that any type of financial and non-financial shock to the SOEs will have a profound effect on the government treasury, and vice versa.

In case of Pakistan, the government's support to the SOEs in the form of subsidies amounted to 203 billion rupees while foreign and domestic loans equaled to 290 billion rupees in 2019. Privatization stands as a pivotal tool employed to address the substantial fiscal burden faced by Pakistan. The government aims to alleviate the financial strain posed by supporting and funding these entities directly. Privatization offers a means to offload the financial responsibility associated with sustaining public enterprises, thereby potentially reducing the need for government subsidies and decreasing the overall fiscal burden. This strategy not only seeks to enhance operational efficiency within these entities but also tries to lighten the fiscal load, allowing the government to allocate resources more optimally and relieve fiscal pressures.

Figure 4.6 clearly illustrates a significant shift in the fiscal scenario surrounding privatization. Prior to the privatization, the cumulative fiscal burden of the SOEs stood at a substantial $US 3 billion, signifying the weight of financial responsibilities borne by the government in sustaining public enterprises. However, after privatization, a noticeable reduction could be observed, diminishing this fiscal load to $US 1.9 billion. This transformation highlights the efficacy of privatization in lightening the fiscal obligations incurred by the government. The transfer of ownership and management of SOEs to private hands often entails a reduction in the need for direct government subsidies, as the operational efficiency and profit-seeking motive of private ownership can mitigate financial strains. Furthermore, the proceeds generated from the privatization process itself contributes to reducing the fiscal burden since the government uses the funds generated from the sale of SOEs to pay off debts or invest in other areas that require financial support.

Yet, it is noteworthy that even post-privatization, fiscal burden remained there in case of Pakistan. This observation highlights that while privatization has alleviated the burden to a considerable extent, a residual impact still persists, putting a question mark on the efficacy of privatization.

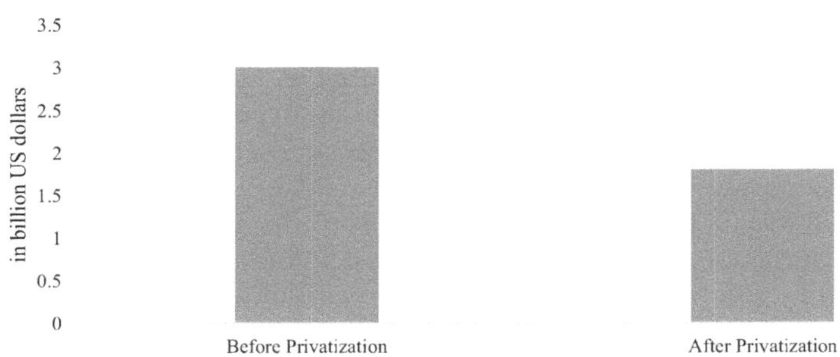

Fig. 4.6 Fiscal Burden of Firms Pre- and Post-Privatization. (*Source*: Based on author's calculations)

Analysis of Selected SOEs after Privatization

In the previous sections we did an overall analysis of state-owned enterprises before and after privatization in terms of their efficiency, performance, and competitiveness. However, the above analysis gave us a very gloomy picture of the public sector. In fact, the pre-privatization era of individual firms represents a debacle of mismanagement and systematic lags. Moreover, lack of incentives and over-governance further added to the fuel and the same pattern continued even after the privatization of many firms. In order to see the effect of privatization on the performance and efficiency of individual firms, we calculated five-year averages of net profit to sales ratio and return on assets (ROAs) before and after privatization of selected firms from various sectors presented in Table 4.1.

The results related to the performance of firms show that out of 19 firms, 5 firms operated on negative profit-to-sales ratio before privatization. Out of these five firms, four of them retained the same status for the next five years, even after privatization. These included Javedan Cement, K-electric, National Motors, and Quality Steel. Furthermore, even those firms which were operating on positive marginal profits before privatization started operating on negative profit margins after privatization. Such firms included Fazal Veg Ghee, Associated Industries, Kakakhel Industries, Metropolitan Steel, Pak Suzuki, Thal Industries, and PVC Ltd.

Furthermore, the results related to pre- and post-privatization efficiency of firms show that majority of the firms presented a better picture in the pre-privatization era as compared to what they did in the post-privatization era. Even some of the entities in the power, construction, and manufacturing sectors maintained negative return on assets even after privatization. The average ROA shows a decrease of more than 50% in post-privatization time as compared to the pre-privatization time. The analysis shows that 5 out of 19 firms in the sample have a negative ROA before privatization whereas this number increased to 10 after privatization (Fig. 4.7).

Overall results show that in terms of efficiency after privatization, only Al-Ghazi, Javedan Cement, National Refinery, and Sindh Alkal showed improved efficiency. While in terms of performance, Al-Ghazi, Attock Refinery, National Refinery, Sindh Alkal, and Bolan showed improvement.

Table 4.1 Pre- and Post-privatization analysis of firms

Firms		*Before Privatization*		*After Privatization*	
		Performance	*Efficiency*	*Performance*	*Efficiency*
	Sectors	Net Profit/ Sale (Average Five years)	ROA	Net Profit/ Sale (Average Five year)	ROA
Al Ghazi Tractors Ltd.	Manufacturing, Mining & Engineering	1.5	0.2	4.8	1.2
Attock refinery	Capital Market Transactions	1.84	2.6	2.6	−0.3
Fazal Veg Ghee	Ghee	3.32	0.4	−8.7	0.2
Associated Industries	Ghee	5.22	1.2	−0.68	−1.6
Javedan Cement	Cement Industry	−1. 12	−0.001	−8.0	0.4
KESC	Power and Energy	−28. 18	−0.1	−18.7	−0.1
Kakakhel Industries	Ghee	4.48	1.6	−2.52	−0.4
Metropolitan Steel	Manufacturing, Mining & Engineering	3.1	0.3	−33.14	−0.5
Millat Tractors	Manufacturing, Mining & Engineering	3.78	0.4	3.76	0.4
National Motors	Manufacturing, Mining & Engineering	−7.62	−2.0	−32.04	−0.3
National refinery	Oil and Gas	4. 18	0.8	4.88	2.3
PTC	Telecommunication	39.8	0.3	27.07	0.2
Pak Suzuki	Manufacturing, Mining & Engineering	5. 14	2.0	−2.26	−0.02
Quality Steel	Manufacturing, Mining & Engineering	−5.84	−0.06	−12.2	−0.05
Sindh Alkal	Chemical	4.92	0.08	18. 1	0.1
Thal Industries Corporation		13.5	0.54	−4.06	−0.03

(*continued*)

Table 4.1 (continued)

Firms		*Before Privatization*		*After Privatization*	
		Performance	*Efficiency*	*Performance*	*Efficiency*
Zeal Pak	Cement	146.04	0.21	1.84	0.07
Bolan	Automobile/Textile	−17.52	−0.01	4.62	0.15
PVC Ltd	Chemical	3.8	0.2	−71.5	−0.45

Source: Authors' calculations based on data from Federal Footprint: SOEs Performance Review by Finance Division, GoP

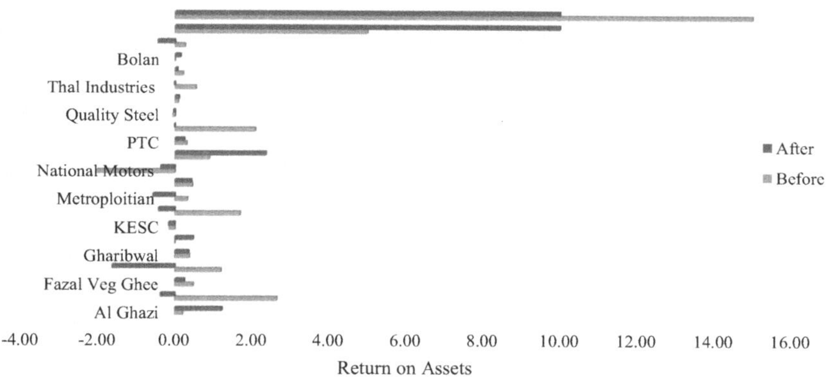

Fig. 4.7 Efficiency of Selected Firms in Pre- and Post-Privatization (Five Year Averages). (*Source*: Author's analysis based on data from companies' annual reports)

Concluding Remarks

Considering the dismal financial situation of SOEs, we proposed privatization of these SOEs as an alternative policy solution. However, we needed to dig deeper into the pre- and post-privatization position of these SOEs in order to get a final verdict on privatization being the optimal solution. Therefore, in this chapter, we assessed the pre- and post-privatization scenario of firms in terms of performance, efficiency, and competitiveness using some more indicators. These included net profit-to-sales ratio, returns on assets, concentration ratios, and change in the relative prices.

Aggregated analysis of the firms shows improvement in their performance and a slight decline in the fiscal burden. The efficiency and competitiveness of firms also experienced slight improvement. However, this improvement is insufficient to make a strong ground for privatization.

Even after analyzing a number of selected firms individually, it is concluded that privatization does not lead to any significant improvement in the performance, efficiency, and competitiveness of the SOEs. In fact, the situation of most of the firms showed further deterioration, attributed to structural inefficiencies which remain intact not only at the governance level but also at the delivery level. Therefore, we conclude that slight improvements in these indicators cannot make a ground for large-scale privatization. Hence, privatization cannot be used as the only fix for the problems related to SOEs in an under-developing country like Pakistan. A more prudent course of action is needed where we need to unravel the intricate dynamics at play within SOEs and during the different stages of their privatization. For this, a careful empirical analysis will help in understanding the various factors that could either slow down or magnify the expected advantages of privatization. Thus, the forthcoming chapter will center its attention on conducting empirical analysis, aiming to unearth further insights regarding the stance of privatization. Through this rigorous examination, we will look deeper into the subject, uncovering additional factors that might contribute to our understanding of the privatization paradigm.

References

Abdullahi, Y. Z., & Mohammed, Y. (2012). Privatization and firm performance: An empirical study of selected privatized firms in Nigeria. *Mediterranean Journal of Social Sciences, 3*(11), 207–220.

D'Souza, J., Megginson, W., & Nash, R. (2005). Effect of institutional and firm-specific characteristics on post-privatization performance: Evidence from developed countries. *Journal of Corporate Finance, 11*(5), 747–766.

Georganou, A. (2015). *Firms' performance pre- and post-privatization*, School of Economics and Business Administration, International Hellenic University.

Okten, C., & Arin, K. P. (2006). The effects of privatization on efficiency: How does privatization work? *World Development, 34*(9), 1537–1556.

Omran, M. (2004). The performance of state-owned enterprises and newly privatized firms: Does privatization really matter? *World Development, 32*(6), 1019–1041.

Salawu, R. O., & Akinlo, O. O. (2005). Privatization and efficiency: Evaluation of corporate financial performance. *Journal of Social Sciences, 10*(3), 171–180.

Shi, W., & Sun, J. (2016). The impact of privatization on efficiency and profitability: Evidence from Chinese listed firms, 2001–2010. *Economics of Transition, 24*(3), 393–420.

Tsamenyi, M., Onumah, J., & Tetteh-Kumah, E. (2010). Post-privatization performance and organizational changes: Case studies from Ghana. *Critical Perspectives on Accounting, 21*(5), 428–442.

CHAPTER 5

Pre- and Post-privatization Performance of Soes: An Empirical Analysis

Abstract The main motive of this book is to assess the impacts of privatization in Pakistan, compared to exploratory, the empirical analysis is a more scientific and comprehensive way to examine the evaluation of privatized SOEs. Chapter 5 conducts a thorough empirical analysis of the privatized SOEs by involving difference-in-difference approach. Setting up the before and after outcomes, we analyze the impact of privatization on firm performance, and efficiency, and highlight the sector-specific outcomes. The findings reveal mixed results: while some privatized firms show some improvement in performance and efficiency compared to their pre-privatization state, while overall it is not significant. However, there is a notable improvement in the efficiency of privatized firms in terms of return on assets (ROA). Sector-specific analysis uncovers varied impacts of privatization, with some sectors experiencing positive effects while others remain relatively unchanged. The chapter underscores the importance of an enabling regulatory environment to support successful privatization efforts, emphasizing the need for effective regulation to ensure the efficient operation of privatized entities within a competitive market framework.

Keywords Comparative analysis of privatization • Sectoral analysis • Profitability • Subsidies analysis • Economic efficiency

G. Samad, N. Faraz, *The Face of Privatization in Pakistan*,
https://doi.org/10.1007/978-981-97-8385-4_5

In the preceding chapters, we thoroughly examined the challenging circumstances faced by SOEs in Pakistan. Thus, we hypothesized that privatization could serve as a viable solution. However, this chapter which involved analyzing the performance, efficiency, and competitiveness of SOEs both before and after privatization has thoroughly examined the situation with an empirical lens to gain a better understanding of this subject.

Since there is a lack of pre- and post-privatization empirical analysis in case of Pakistan. Therefore, in this chapter, we dug deeper into analysis. Through the application of empirical analysis and a comprehensive study of case studies spanning various industries, we have attempted to gain a more profound understanding. Our principal aim is to formulate a final verdict on the suitability of privatization to get insights on informed privatization policies.

Effects of Privatization on Firm Performance and Efficiency

We start with our empirical analysis[1] by looking into the performance of privatized SOEs in Pakistan. Our objective is to scrutinize their performance and efficiency, with a view to determine whether privatization has led to an enhancement in their overall performance.

In developing countries, proceeds from privatization typically go to the government instead of being reinvested in the privatized firms (Megginson, 2005). In Pakistan, the government has similarly used these funds to reduce the fiscal deficit rather than reinvesting in other industries. Literature suggests that privatizing profitable firms first can increase sales proceeds (Megginson et al., 2004; Gupta et al., 2008). In this context, we observe a positive relationship between profitability and the privatization decision. Conversely, the literature also indicates that unprofitable enterprises show significant efficiency improvements following privatization, suggesting a negative relationship between profitability and privatization. Thus, the relative importance placed by the government matters.

Privatization is generally unpopular among the population and carries political risks for politicians, who may delay the process to avoid these risks. This trend is evident in Pakistan. We examine the political economy of privatization to test its political determinants. It is widely observed that politicians target public funds to regions with swing voters to win elections, often using politically connected firms and public enterprises to

[1] The details of the econometric technique and data are provided in the Appendix A.

create more jobs in those areas (Cox & McCubbins, 1986; Persson & Tabellini, 2002).

Further, donor conditionalities could impact the privatization process in Pakistan. The government often uses fund programs to overcome economic difficulties, with PSE reforms, including pricing, subsidies, and privatization, being one of the conditions (IMF, 2018). This conditionality can hasten the privatization process without proper reforms (Breen & Doyle, 2013).

To address these concerns, we use appropriate methodology (the two-stage least square [2SLS]) to measure the refine effect of privatization on firm performance (results are reported in Table 5.2). Following Serdar and Nandani (2011), in the first stage, we use financial and political variables as instruments for privatization, then in second stage, we estimate the impact of privatization on post-privatization performance.

In Table 5.1, we present the alternative outcomes of the firm performance is determined as the ratio of Profits/Sales which is fairly established

Table 5.1 Effects of Privatization on Firm Performance

	Δ *in Profit/Sales*	Δ *in Profit/Sales*	Δ *in Profit/Sales*	Δ *in Profit/Sales*
	(1)	(2)	(3)	(4)
Privatization	0.863	0.863	0.863	0.863
	(0.911)	(0.911)	(0.911)	(0.911)
Ln (Sales)	−3.474	−3.474	−3.474	−3.474
	(3.652)	(3.652)	(3.652)	(3.652)
Profit/Sales	0.417***	0.417***	0.417***	0.417***
	(0.063)	(0.063)	(0.063)	(0.063)
Urbanization	–	–	–	
Firm size	0.675	0.675	0.675	0.675
	(2.278)	(2.278)	(2.278)	(2.278)
Donor Effect		0.004	0.004	0.004
		(0.005)	(0.005)	(0.005)
Democracy			7.877	7.877
			(9.881)	(9.881)
Competitive Election				15.551 (9.587)
R^2	0.25	0.25	0.25	0.25
Industry FE	Yes	Yes	Yes	Yes
Firm FE	Yes	Yes	Yes	Yes
City FE	Yes	Yes	Yes	Yes
Number of firms	48	48	48	48
Number of firm-year	1096	1096	1096	1096

Source: Based on Author's Analysis

Table 5.2 Effects of Privatization on the Efficiency of Firms

	Δ *in* *ROA*	Δ *in* *ROA*	Δ *in* *Ln Sales*
	(1)	(2)	(3)
Privatization	0.740**	0.740**	−0.088
	(0.394)	(0.394)	(0.055)
Ln (Sales)	−0.146	−0.160	0.002
	(0.130)	(0.130)	(0.011)
Profit/Sales	0.002	0.002	0.002*
	(0.003)	(0.003)	(0.001)
Urbanization	–	–	
Firm Importance	−0.139		
	(0.189)		
Donor Effect	0.003		−0.091
	(0.241)		(0.121)
Democracy	−1.064*		−0.062
	(0.610)		(0.093)
Competitive Election			
R^2	0.12	0.12	0.16
Industry FE	Yes	Yes	Yes
Firm FE	Yes	Yes	Yes
City FE	Yes	Yes	Yes
Number of firms	48	48	48
Number of firm-year	1096	1096	1096

Source: Based on Author's Analysis

indicator in literature to examine the performance of the firms. From columns 1 to 4, we note that privatized firms experience a mild increase in their performance as compared to their pre-privatization period. However, this difference in performance is not significant. We consider all other influencer including financial and political risk indicators and firm characteristics such as the year, industry, city, and the state effects.

For instance, the industry and year effects are included to control the industry-level differences and changes in macroeconomic policy. City effects are considered to capture the differences in location of the firms. Similarly, the timing of elections and conditions set by donors also included to refine the analysis. It shows these do not appear to have any discernible impact on the performance of privatized SOEs in post-privatization period.

For efficiency of the firms, we use the rate of return indicator which is measures return on their assets (ratio of profit-to-sales), results given in

Table 5.2. We note that privatization increases the efficiency of the privatized firms compared to government-owned firms, this difference is significant at the 5% level of significance. We also look at whether privatization increases the efficiency of the firms in terms of increased sales. The results in the column (3) show that privatization does not enhance the efficiency of the privatized firms in terms of the increased sales, rather it has declined after privatization. However, a slight improvement in the efficiency of firms in terms of increased sales has been through an increase in the profit to sales ratio.

Early Post-Privatization Effects of Profitable SOEs

To ensure that our findings are consistent, we extend our analysis to investigate the effects of privatization in the early stages of privatization. In doing so, we limit our dataset to a timeframe of five years prior and post-privatization for PSEs. The results can be found in Table 5.3 which presents an insightful comparison between fully government-owned firms versus those underwent privatization. Upon closer examination, it becomes evident that although there is a slight improvement in productivity within privately owned firms as compared to their governmental counterparts, this difference does not hold any statistical significance. The same pattern emerges when considering efficiency indicators between these two groups—no significant differences were observed.

Effects of Financial and Political Factors on the Privatization Decision

The decision to privatize a firm is influenced by a myriad of factors, including financial variables, firm characteristics, and political variables. In order to address this issue and gain a comprehensive understanding of this phenomenon, we undertook two analyses. First, we investigated whether financial and political factors played any pivotal role in shaping decisions around privatization. Second, we utilized instrumental variable method which allowed us to employ two-stage least squares analysis as an effective approach for addressing endogeneity within the context of privatization process.

Table 5.3 Early post-privatization effects: Assessment using data restricted to five years before-after period

	Δ *Profits/Sales*	Δ *Profits/Sales*	Δ *Profits/Sales*	Δ *ROA*	Δ *ROA*	Δ *Ln (sales)*	Δ *Ln (sales)*
	(1)	(2)	(3)	(4)	(5)	(6)	(7)
Privatization	0.326	0.187	0.507	0.089	0.410	−0.033	−0.106
	(1.462)	(2.110)	(0.814)	(0.499)	(1.042)	(0.021)	(0.133)
Industry FE	Yes	Yes	Yes	Yes	No	Yes	No
Firm FE	Yes	Yes	Yes	Yes	Yes	Yes	Yes
Years FE	Yes	Yes	Yes	Yes	No	Yes	Yes
Number of Firms	48	48	48	48	48	48	48
Number of firm-year	777	777	777	777	509	777	777

Source: Based on Author's Analysis

Table 5.4 exhibits the results of the analysis investigating the influence of financial and political elements on the privatization decision. The first three columns indicate that firms with higher profitability exhibit a reduced likelihood of privatization, and this correlation is statistically significant. It implies that profitability does not considerably impede or accelerate decision-making processes. Moreover, the ratio of a firm's sales in relation to the total sales of all the government-owned firms also plays a significant role in determining the government's decision to privatize the firms.

While taking the privatization decisions, it is also crucial to take into consideration the impact that firms of national importance have on the privatization decision. Interestingly enough, our findings indicate that firms deemed as having higher levels of national importance are less likely to undergo this process of privatization. However, this effect is insignificant. This pattern aligns with current narrative surrounding several such organizations including Pakistan International Airlines (PIA) and others

Table 5.4 Effects of financial and political factors on the privatization decision

	(1)	*(2)*	*(3)*	*(4)*	*(5)*
Ln (Sales)	0.406**	0.397**	0.385**	0.406**	0.406**
	(0.195)	(0.193)	(0.193)	(0.187)	(0.187)
Net Profit/Sales	−0.016**	−0.016**	−0.015**	−0.016**	−0.016**
	(0.006)	(0.006)	(0.006)	(0.006)	(0.006)
Urbanization	−0.135	−0.130	−0.131	−0.162	−0.162
	(0.127)	(0.127)	(0.127)	(0.132)	(0.132)
Firm Importance	−11.326	−11.372	−10.301	−9.539	−9.539
	(10.803)	(10.850)	(10.398)	(9.564)	(9.564)
Donor Effect		−0.0003	−0.0003	−0.0003	−0.0003
		(0.0003)	(0.0003)	(0.0003)	(0.0003)
Democracy			0.220	0.390	0.390
			(0.508)	(0.729)	(0.729)
Competitive Election					0.390
					(0.729)
Gov Vote Share				−3.459	−3.459
				(2.501)	(2.501)
Industry FE	Yes	Yes	Yes	Yes	No
Firm FE	Yes	Yes	Yes	Yes	Yes
Years FE	Yes	Yes	Yes	Yes	No
Number of Firms	48	48	48	48	48
Number of firm-year	777	777	777	777	509

Source: Based on Author's Analysis

like it. As we examine these cases more closely, it becomes evident that the government has encountered immense resistance when attempting to implement measures for their privatization despite multiple attempts over time.

Upon careful analysis of the data presented in columns 4 and 5, it can be observed that there is no significant impact of political factors on privatization. Despite having competitive elections and a certain percentage of government vote share, these variables do not seem to have any tangible effect on privatization outcomes. Interestingly enough, our findings suggest that the decision to privatize particular firms over others does not appear to hinge significantly on electoral considerations—a result which provides further insight into the complexities involved in such policy decisions at higher levels of government.

We also examined the intricate relationship between donor programs and democratic institutions in regards to the privatization of Public Sector Enterprises (PSEs). Donor programs frequently impose conditionalities that require the privatization of SOEs while seeking loans from them. This correlation is represented by our variable, Donor Conditionality Effect, which takes on a value of 1 if an IMF program was present within both the previous and current year—otherwise it holds a zero value. Interestingly enough, our findings suggest that neither democratic regimes nor donor conditionalities have immediate effects on decisions related to PSE privatizations. These results are also aligned with those reported by the IMF in their assessment from 2019, where they concluded that Fund's reform conditionality regarding PSEs were often either unfulfilled or delayed altogether Faraz & Samad (2022), Hakro & Akram (2009), Kouser et al. (2012), Munir & Naqvi (2017), Naqvi & Kemal (2002), Pasha (2014).

Sectoral Analysis

In order to have an interesting view of the success and failure of privatization at sector level, a segregated analysis of all the sectors has also been conducted. Such an analysis is important due to two reasons. First, it may provide an interesting picture of the privatization effects. Second, it may provide us with the differences in effects across the sectors due to differences in the nature of the sectors and pre-privatization conditions of each sector.

Using within firm variation, we analyze the change in returns on assets (ΔROA) to assess the performance of the PSEs after the privatization. Columns 1–8 in Table 5.5 show that five sectors (Engineering, Telecom,

Table 5.5 Effects of privatization: Sector-specific success versus failure stories

	Energy Sector	*Engineering Sector*	*Cement Sector*	*Telecom Sector*	*Textile Sector*	*Ghee Indus*	*Chemical Sector*	*Automobile Sector*
	(1)	*(2)*	*(3)*	*(4)*	*(5)*	*(6)*	*(7)*	*(8)*
Privatization	−0.159	0.387	−0.242*	1.023***	9.759***	2.491	−0.099	0.053
	(0.244)	(0.307)	(0.145)	(0.183)	(0.948)	(2.800)	(0.245)	(1.587)
Firm FE	Yes	Yes	Yes	Yes	Yes	Yes	Yes	Yes
Year-State FE	Yes	Yes	Yes	Yes	Yes	Yes	Yes	Yes
R-squared	0.26	0.26	0.40	0.83	0.86	0.27	0.44	0.21
Observations	203	88	112	19	19	131	74	133

Source: Based on Author's Analysis

Textile, Ghee, and Automobile) experienced positive effects of privatization, however, the effect was positive and statistically significant only for the Telecom and Textile sectors. It implies that PSEs in these sectors performed better compared to their pre-privatization period. In contrast, energy, cement, and chemical industries experienced negative effects in their productivity in terms of the returns on the assets. However, the effects of privatization on the cement sector were the worst and statistically significant as compared to the energy and chemical sector.

Concluding Remarks

After uncovering a range of important insights regarding the privatization experience of SOEs in Pakistan, it has been concluded that privatization did not bring big changes in their overall performance. However, positive impact on their operational efficiency has been observed considering how well they used their assets to generate returns. On the contrary, the way they increase their sales didn't seem to get better with privatization.

Looking at specific sectors, it has been observed that privatization has a positive impact on telecom and textile sectors. But on the cement industry, privatization has a negative impact. The rest of the sectors didn't seem to be significantly affected by privatization.

Summing up, our examination reveals that privatization has brought some improvements in few small size sectors while leaving others relatively unchanged. However, it is important to note that lack of enabling environment and a malfunctioning regulatory mechanism were fundamental reasons for privatization which lingered on even after privatization. The over-regulation with lingering controls has not supported its success in Pakistan as regulations are often captured by powerful market players or politicians who prioritize their political gains rather than correcting market failures. As such, an effective regulatory environment remains critical in ensuring that privatized entities continue to operate efficiently within a competitive framework, ultimately benefiting all stakeholders involved.

References

Breen, M., & Doyle, D. (2013). The determinants of privatization: A comparative analysis of developing countries. *Journal of Comparative Policy Analysis: Research and Practice, 15*(1), 1–20.

Cox, G. W., & McCubbins, M. D. (1986). Electoral politics as a redistributive game. *The Journal of Politics, 48*(2), 370–389.

Faraz, N., & Samad, G. (2022). Public Sector Enterprises (PSEs) in Post-Privatization: Evidence from Pakistan. *Journal of Applied Economics, 25*(1), 1239–1259.

Gupta, N., Ham, J., & C. Svejnar, Jan. (2008). Priorities and sequencing in privatization: Evidence from Czech firm panel data. *European Economic Review, 52*(2).

Hakro, A. N., & Akram, M. (2009). Pre-Post performance assessment of privatization process in Pakistan. *International Review of Business Research Papers, 5*(1), 70–86.

IMF. (2018). *2018 review of program design and conditionality*. IMF Executive Board's Review Study.

Kouser, R., Azid, T., & Ali, K. (2012). Financial and operating performance of privatized firms: A case study of Pakistan. *International Research Journal of Finance and Economics, 87*(87), 90–116.

Megginson, W. L. (2005). The economics of bank Privatization. *Journal of Banking and Finance, 29*(1), 1931–1980.

Megginson, W. L., Robert C. N., Jeffry M. N., & Annette B. P. (2004). The choice of private versus public capital markets: Evidence from privatizations. *The Journal of Finance, 59*(6), 2835–2870.

Munir, K., & Naqvi, N. (2017). Privatization in the land of believers: The political economy of privatization in Pakistan. *Modern Asian Studies, 51*(6), 1695–1726.

Naqvi, S. N. H., & Kemal, A. R. (2002). Privatization, efficiency and employment in Pakistan. In *How does privatization work?* (pp. 244–267). Routledge.

Pasha, Y. (2014). *"The Privatization Program in Pakistan" Social Policy and Development Center, Policy Brief No. 24.*

Persson, T., & Tabellini, G. (2002). *Political economics: Explaining economic policy*. MIT Press.

Serdar, D., & Nandani, G. (2011). The decision to privatise: Finance and politics. *The Journal of Finance, LXVI*(1), 241–269.

PART III

Case Studies of Privatization in Pakistan

Pakistan is among those developing nations that has enthusiastically embraced neoliberalism and fully adopted *Washington Consensus* policies, making it an interesting empirical site to study why privatization, despite its recurrent failures, is still adored. Countless researches have been done to find out answer to questions related to the success of privatization, but the reality is that there does not exist any full-fledged consensus in favor of privatization.

Our analysis also gives us a gloomy picture of the impact of privatization; however, anecdotal evidence suggests that there have been some success stories as well. In this regard, dissecting individual case studies within various sectors in the context of privatization is of high significance. Since each sector possesses its distinct dynamics and challenges that intersect with the privatization process in unique ways. Therefore, by exploring separate case studies, we can gain a magnified perspective on how privatization manifests within each sector. This approach allows us to appreciate the diversity of outcomes that privatization can yield, ranging from success stories to instances of suboptimal gains.

In the subsequent chapters, we will try to figure out how our privatization experience has turned out in case of some of the major entities within the power, manufacturing, telecommunication, and financial sectors. These include K-electric, DG Cement, Maple Leaf Cement, Kohat Cement, Pakistan Telecommunications Company Limited, Allied Bank Limited, and Habib Bank Limited.

CHAPTER 6

Power Sector: A Case Study of K-Electric

Abstract Amidst operational inefficiencies and financial struggles, K-Electric (formerly KESC) faced substantial challenges necessitating its privatization in 2005. Chapter 6 provides an in-depth case study of K-Electric (formerly KESC), tracing its history from its origins as a private entity to its nationalization and eventual privatization. Following its privatization, the efforts made by the new management, particularly the Abraaj Group, to improve K-Electric's performance through capital injection and operational reforms. However, despite these efforts, K-Electric has struggled to achieve sustained profitability and address systematic issues such as transmission and distribution losses. Despite some improvements in operational efficiency, K-Electric remains ineffective in meeting Karachi's energy demands efficiently. Thus, this chapter underscores the need for further analysis and intervention to address the challenges facing K-Electric and the power sector in Pakistan, emphasizing the importance of sustainable solutions to ensure reliable and affordable energy supply for the residents of Karachi.

Keywords Inefficiencies • Privatization of K-Electric • Case study of K-Electric • Transmission and distribution losses • Power Sector in Pakistan

G. Samad, N. Faraz, *The Face of Privatization in Pakistan*, https://doi.org/10.1007/978-981-97-8385-4_6

Karachi, with a population exceeding 20 million, is one of the most populous urban areas globally. The metropolitan is acknowledged as Pakistan's financial hub and industrial center. Following partition in 1947, Karachi, as the industrial nucleus and capital of the nation, experienced a remarkable surge in industrialization. This led to a significant escalation in the demand for electric power. Between 1947 and 1956, the consumer base doubled, with residential and industrial sales surging by five and eight times, respectively. Particularly noteworthy was the substantial increase in industrial consumption, soaring from 6 million KWh in 1948 to 50 million KWh by 1957.[1]

Karachi Electric Supply Company (KESC), a private entity before independence, is mainly responsible for the production and distribution of electricity within the city of Karachi and its vicinities. While it produces and distributes electrical power to Karachi, its provision of electricity to consumers in the neighboring towns in Sindh and Balochistan Provinces is not widely recognized.

History

To address the power requirements of a tiny port town called Karachi, the Karachi Electric Supply Company (KESC) was established in 1913 under the Indian Companies Act, 1882, as a privately owned enterprise. Before the government took control of its operations in 1952, its financial performance was satisfactory. However, the company's net earnings dropped due to fuel cost increases, leading to the suspension of dividends. GOP intervened and acquired majority control by purchasing 51% of outstanding shares. Generation capacity within KESC increased significantly from 1947 to 1956. Its power producing capacity was around 60 MW which was raised to 119 MW in 1959 with the establishment of Water and Power Development Authority (WAPDA). The company's financial situation improved in 1953 with substantial rate increases and resumed dividend payments.

Generation Capacity within KESC during the 1950s and 1960s

In 1952, when GOP assumed control of KESC, its power generation assets comprised an outdated diesel plant generating 6 MW, alongside two steam plants. These included an old station producing 23.5 MW and a

[1] KESC Power Project, IBRD, 1958.

newer facility with two units each generating 30 MW. The transmission network spanned 48 miles of 66 KV overhead lines, 4.3 miles of underground cables, and included 4 substations. Additionally, the medium voltage grid covered about 200 miles, with a low voltage distribution system spanning 460 miles, hosting a total transformer capacity of 89,000 KVa.

By the early 1960s, KESC's generation capacity had expanded to 247 MW from steam plants and a dwindling 25 MW from the aging diesel plant, reducing to an effective 20 MW. The primary steam plants were located at Karachi "B" and Karachi "C," with capacities of 115 MW and 152 MW, respectively. The diesel plants were situated at Elander Road and the Sindh Industrial Trading Estate (SITE), with effective capacities of 4 MW and 16 MW, respectively.

The transmission system comprised an inner 132 KV ring main grid, linking Korangi power station to key substations, and a double circuit 132 KV spur line to Dhabeji and Gharo, connecting Hyderabad and the country. A secondary 66 KV ring main grid encircled the city, linking diesel stations and West Wharf to the 132 KV grid. High-tension distribution operated at 11 KV, with most lines underground. However, over 900 miles of the 1400 V low-tension system were overhead, particularly burdened in the city center, prompting rehabilitation efforts and 11 KV system reinforcement to avert short circuits.[2]

Financial Scenario in the 1950s and 1960s

KESC's financial performance has generally been positive, although there was a decrease in earnings in 1952 and 1953 due to fluctuations in fuel prices and the inability to offset this through an increase in tariffs. As a result, the company's net earnings dropped significantly, leading to a suspension of dividend payments. However, this situation improved in 1953 with substantial rate increases, enabling the resumption of dividend payments. The dividends for 1953 and 1954 were at 6%, which increased to 7% in 1955 and further to 7.5% in 1956.[3]

The trend of increasing energy sales persisted until a decline in 1965, notably in the industrial sector due to conflicts between Pakistan and India. Average revenue per KWh fluctuated between 12.1 to 13.9 paisa (US 2.5–2.9 cents). Despite a doubling of gross revenues, operating

[2] Annual Developmental Program, Pakistan, 1958 and 1967.

[3] Planning Commission of Pakistan, 1957.

expenses rose only by 1.6 times, attributed to reduced fuel and operational costs per KWh. The rate of return, complying with the rate covenant, ranged from 11.8 to 14.2% from 1960 to 1964, decreasing to 10.3% in 1965. KESC declared cash dividends of 10% until 1962, subsequently issuing 10% stock dividends in 1963 and 1964, charged against the Special 15BB Tax Reserve. In August 1966, a combination of 6% cash and 4% stock dividends was declared. Tax concessions aimed at promoting plant expansion included a four-year tax holiday for profits from new facilities before July 1, 1965, and a two-year tax holiday for those placed in service between July 1, 1965, and June 30, 1970, along with accelerated depreciation for tax deferment. Operating losses for tax purposes were common, offset by future taxable income, resulting in tax liabilities only in 1962 and 1965.

KESC in 1970s

Until 1970, KESC exhibited effectiveness and competency. However, following this period, the company's performance declined due to ineffective management and high transmission and distribution losses, thereby posing a financial risk to the company. The trend of industrial growth with a significant rise in industrial consumption also experienced a setback after the 1970s. There was a gradual decrease in the percentage share of industrial consumption from 1970 onward, with a noticeable drop of 14% recorded over ten years from 1970 to 1980.

Box 6.1 Sources of Power Generation in Pakistan

Renewable Sources

Hydro (2nd largest source of generation)
Wind
Solar
Bagasse

Non-renewable Sources

Thermal (1st largest source of generation)
Nuclear

The shift in consumption patterns is linked to the adjustments in tariff rates, which resulted in higher rates for industrial consumers compared to domestic users. This gap reached a significant 40 paisa/KWh for industrial consumers and 28 paisa/KWh for domestic consumers by 1979.

In 1970, the Karachi Electric Supply Corporation had a total installed capacity of 392 MW, which was higher than the peak demand of 254 MW. The annual electricity generation stood at 1386 million units, serving 254,225 consumers. The average unit sale price was only PKR. 0.134 with recorded system losses of around 19% during that year. The oil crisis in October 1973, triggered by an oil embargo imposed by OPEC in response to US decisions during the Yom Kippur war, affected KESC's tariff structure. Consequently, the company increased its average tariff by approximately 30% at the beginning of 1974 due to escalating fuel costs.

Between 1971 and 1978, an additional 209,918 consumers were incorporated, while the generation capacity increased by 110 MW in 1977 alone. System losses, which stood at 18% in the 1960s, escalated to 22% by 1977. The Overall Generation Capacity Factor, which was previously 44%, declined to 42%. Financially, from 1972 to 1978, the Net Profit Margin on Sales after Interest plummeted to –0.38%, marking the company's first experience of financial loss. The Return on Capital after Interest also turned negative, reaching –0.23%.

What Went Wrong during the mid-1980s?

Recognizing the reliance on fossil oil for power generation, WAPDA expanded the National Grid Network to connect with KESC's transmission system using 220 KV and 132 KV lines. Despite a 2% increase in installed generation capacity from 521 MW in 1977 to 745 MW in 1980, industrial growth stagnated due to revised rates, resulting in high production costs. Tariff increases were linked to fuel price fluctuations and constraints on gas allocation for KESC's gas turbines. Failure to address gas reserve constraints in the late 1970s exacerbated the energy crisis.

In the 1980s, KESC attempted to meet growing energy demands by commissioning new power plants but neglected efficiency improvements in existing plants and transmission/distribution network upgrades. Despite significant financial allocations, T&D network inefficiencies persisted, leading to deteriorating financial health. Integration into WAPDA in 1985–1986 aimed for more balanced energy management. Despite achieving targets for new customer connections, industrial growth failed to match the 1960s boom. By 1991, energy generation reached 62,929 Wh, with 40% sold to industries and 35% to residential consumers. Peak demand reached 1224 MW annually, with KESC's installed capacity at 1723 MW. Despite plans for modernization, KESC's transmission and distribution infrastructure remained inadequate, contributing to worsening line losses.

KESC during 1990s

The performance of KESC experienced a notable decline, with system losses escalating from 17% in 1985/1986 to 35% in 1996. In response to the company's faltering financial health in 1996, there were discussions regarding its transfer to private ownership. However, in May 1999, management was handed over to the military in hopes of revitalizing operational and financial aspects. Despite efforts, including the induction of army personnel, the situation did not significantly improve. Tariff increases failed to boost revenue due to potential customer migration to self-generation and increased pilferage. ADB's November 2000 report highlighted the ineffectiveness of military involvement and advocated for privatization to address corruption and political interference. KESC deployed army personnel for covert operations to curb illegal connections and management roles. The objective was to reduce T&D losses by 19% over three years, with specific reduction targets set for each year. Despite these measures, the military's involvement from late 1998 did not yield the anticipated outcomes for KESC and WAPDA.

Plans of Privatization of the Power Sector

The stage had been set for the privatization of the power sector with the initiative of the 1994 Power Policy. This policy was created to entice foreign investment. As this was the first time the government had actively sought out a sizeable private investment in the power sector, it provided exceptionally generous and profitable incentives to investors. Before that in 1992, the Strategic Plan for the Privatization of the Power Sector by WAPDA was approved by the government. Making and establishing a regulatory authority to oversee the restructuring process and to control monopolistic practices was the main objective of the strategic plan. As a result, National Electric Power Regulatory Authority (NEPRA) was

Box 6.2 Tariff Rate in 1994 Power Policy

Energy Price	*PKR/KWh*
Fuel	0.621
Variable Operation and Maintenance	0.030
Capacity Price	
Escalable component (fixed operations & maintenance, insurance, administration, return on equity etc.)	0.359
Non-escalable component (debt servicing)	0.822
Foreign Exchange Risk Insurance	0.120
Total tariff	1.952

Source: Ali and Beg (2007)

created under the Regulation of Generation, Transmission and Distribution of Electric Power Act, 1997. It was established to bring a clear and responsible economic regulation, based on ethical business practices, to Pakistan's electricity market. To what extent it got successful in that is a subject which we will hold for later.

Besides, several other projects were also started by the government under the Power Sector Energy Development Programme (PSEDP) in collaboration with the World Bank. Some of the world's most favorable conditions were offered to investors who wanted to install generation capacity in the nation.

According to those conditions, the government had to pay the operational costs of the private power plants, that is, the Independent Power Producers (IPPs) in addition to the rate of return of around 15–18% annually. Furthermore, the Government of Pakistan provided sovereign assurances in the form of guarantees. Additionally, corporate income tax, customs tax, sales tax, and other levies on imported equipment were exempted for Independent Power Producers (IPPs). Aside from a high tariff charge, the IPPs were free to employ any technology—with the exception of big hydroelectric projects on the Indus. Additionally, they had the option to use any primary fuel. All IPPs today are thermal power plants that run on natural gas, high-speed diesel (HSD), or furnace oil.

However, there were three aspects of this policy that stood out. First of all, despite offering incredibly huge profits, it didn't offer any incentives to optimize the plant design. In fact, many thermal IPPs misrepresented their efficiency because the government was covering all the operating expenses. Second, because the policy was fuel-blind, investors were free to build furnace oil-based thermal IPPs, which is the most expensive fuel alternative, knowing that the government would pay for the fuel. Finally, since the government was ensuring investors' returns, there was almost no market competition, which again led to inefficiency.

From KESC to K-Electric: A Privatization Journey

KESC's performance began to decline significantly in the 1990s as it struggled to generate enough cash flow to cover its capital expenditure, debt obligations, and operational expenses. This financial deterioration posed a threat to its operations and had negative implications for the energy sector's viability. Karachi experienced frequent power outages and breakdowns due to KESC's failure to keep up with the increasing demand for electricity, which was growing at an average rate of 8% annually in the late 1990s.

Additionally, KESC's aging and poorly maintained transmission system made it prone to frequent power outages. Finally, it was privatized in 2005 by the Privatization Commission of Pakistan, when KES Power, a Cayman Islands-based business, purchased 66.4% share in KESC. It is the only power company which is vertically integrated and involved in the generation, transmission, and distribution activities within the largest industrial base of the country. For KE, the circumstances significantly deteriorated in FY1996 when net profit margin declined by 2.87%. Following that, KE

Box 6.3 How the name "KE" evolved?

- It was named Incorporation of Karachi Electric Supply Corporation Limited on September 13, 1913.
- It was registered "Karachi Electric Supply Corporation Limited" in 1953 when it was nationalized.
- The name was again changed to "Karachi Electric Supply Company Limited" in 2008.
- For now it is called "K-Electric Limited".

Box 6.4 Shareholders holding 10% or more (as at June 30, 2021)

Government holding	*6726912278 (24.36%)*
Kes power limited	18335542678 (66.40%)

Source: KE Annual Report 2021

began experiencing consistent net losses. Although the decision to privatize KE in 2005 was unpopular domestically, the military administration of that time nonetheless ignored the established protocols. Prior to privatization, KE had significant issues with its governance structure, inadequate financial management, and operational and commercial inefficiencies, which set forth the path for its privatization.

Administrative Control of KESC after Privatization

After privatization in 2005, KES Power purchased a 66.4% share in KE. Al Jomaih Group from Saudi Arabia and Hassan Associates from Pakistan were among the company's first investors. The privatization of KE was considered flawed from the outset because neither of the companies had any significant expertise in managing electric utilities, much less a vertically integrated electric company of such size and complexity. Therefore, the Al Jomaih group started searching for an exit strategy due to continued and significant losses.

KES Power was thus taken over by a few private equity funds associated with the Abraaj Group (Dubai-based Company) in 2009. The new Abraaj-led KESC management injected much-needed capital, implemented reforms such as rightsizing/downsizing, implemented a ruthless policy of continuous load-shedding repeatedly per day in "high-loss areas," and ran its power plants on cheaper gas rather than expensive furnace oil. Hence, for the first time in nearly two decades, the company was able to overcome its losses and return a profit. Abraaj Group appeared to be a huge success to outsiders because, in 2018, it was in charge of managing more than $13 billion in assets. Nonetheless, there was an unquestionable evidence in the public domain that shows that the Abraaj Group lost control of KE as early as 2018.

By 2015 and continuing afterward, Abraaj Holdings and Abraaj Investment Management, according to the US Securities and Exchange Commission (SEC), "were bankrupt, lacking the legitimate income to fund basic expenses of the business such as workers' wages and other operational costs." The Abraaj Group finally fell behind on its loan payments in the beginning of 2018, which caused two of its creditors to pursue a court-supervised restructuring.

The Grand Court of the Cayman Islands appointed Price Water house Coopers (PWC) as an interim liquidator of Abraaj Holdings and Deloitte as an interim liquidator of Abraaj Investment Management. Certain assets of the Abraaj Group are now under the management of new people. These changes had significant legal repercussions for KE. Since 2018, KE has been a floundering ship, which accounts for its dreadful performance. All governments keep a tight eye on businesses operating in sensitive sectors. Why did GoP permit liquidators to gain control of KE, one could only wonder?

Privatization of KESC: Success or Failure?

KESC had clearly been among the worst affected state-run businesses, with negative gross margins since the end of the 1990s. The company's cost for producing electricity was always more than its income. This has been occurring as a result of widespread electricity theft, constant and consistent transmission and distribution losses, obsolete machinery and transmission facilities, power failures, load shedding, a small number of connected customers, and a high allocation of questionable receivables from government each year Jamil et al. (2022), Qazi & Jahanzaib (2018), Tiep et al. (2021), Ullah et al. (2017).

At the end of 2004, the Transmission and Distribution Losses were 37.80%, the plant and machinery's expected lifetime had decreased by almost 60%, and KESC had lost nearly 3.6 billion PKR in profits over a period of three years as a result of write-offs against provision for questionable debts. The corporation held an additional 2.25 billion PKR in provisions against questionable receivables in 2004, bringing the total provisioning against questionable debts to a whopping 8.93 billion PKR.

The government took major initiatives in reviving KESC including heavy subsidies of 17.572 billion PKR during 2003 and 2004. Special grants were also provided from the PSDP during these years amounting to around more than 2.5 billion PKR. In order to minimize the T&D losses, the government had agreed to invest in a project which required an investment of 13.698 billion PKR which was to be funded out of the PSDP fund. But sustaining and subsidizing the annual losses of KESC every year was a sunk cost for the GoP.

In view of all this, the proposal to privatize KESC was put on the table which took many years to materialize. However, questions arise in mind, do we see any significant improvement in the performance of such an important utility for the nation's largest industrial base after privatization. Do we see any validity for the government's justifications for the privatization of the KESC? Is there any noticeable improvement in the generational capacity of the company? Do we witness any significant decrease in the T&D losses? Is there any decrease in the receivables from the government in the form of subsidy (termed as tariff adjustment)? Answering all these questions will make one able to judge whether the privatization of KESC a success or a failure. An important point to be noted here is that the success of a utility company cannot be judged only through the net profit/loss scenario of that company. The true judgment about the performance can be made by analyzing the extent of service/utility delivery to its customers. Let us try to find answers to all these questions one by one.

Generation Capacity

The operational performance of K-electric is measured in terms of the number of units it generates in kilowatt per hour (KWH). Before privatization, in 2004, it was able to generate 9274 million KWH. After its privatization in 2005, this figure increased but not to the extent it was expected. After reaching its highest in 2021 (10,938 million KWH), it declined again in 2022 to 8496 million KWH, which is clearly less than what it was before its privatization. This decrease in the generational capacity is more than 8%. Thus, despite being a private entity, it has failed to significantly improve its capacity in terms of power generation (Fig. 6.1).

The chairman NEPRA also expressed his disappointment over the performance of DISCOs including K-electric. The reason for this disappointing performance is that our power generation is dependent upon expensive imported furnace oil. However, despite having sufficient installed production capacity, KE was unable to increase its generation capacity due to lack of funds/foreign reserves to purchase expensive fuel (furnace fuel) for power generation. Alternatively, KE has to rely on gas supplies to fire up their turbines. However, in March 2018, a request for increased gas supplies by KE from Sui Southern Gas Company (SSGC) was denied which

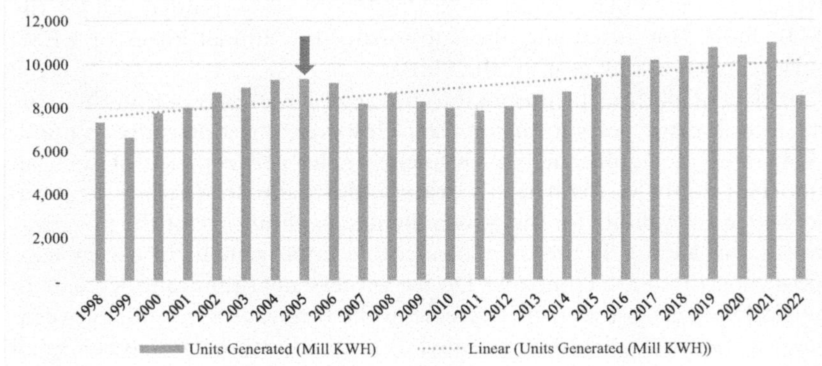

Fig. 6.1 Units Generated (Mill KWH). (*Source*: Based on data taken from Annual Reports of K-Electric, 2007–2022)

put a halt on some of its turbines. Even NEPRA could not mediate into the matter due to its limited role in the supply of fuel which shows weakness of NEPRA as a regulatory body. The reasons put forth by SSGC included restricted supplies from the field and outstanding payments owed to KE.

In short, generation capacity of KE depends on consistent supply of fuel which is a serious policy matter. If on one hand, the use of expensive imported furnace oil as fuel is discouraged to save the foreign reserves, the availability of cheap options in the form of gas supplies (or other renewable fuel options) must be ensured to provide uninterrupted power supply to the people of Karachi.

Net Profit/Loss Scenario

One of the factors leading toward the privatization of KESC was its loss-making situation under state control. The entity was considered as inefficient on one hand and technology deficient on the other. The net profit/loss figure is achieved after subtracting the cost of electricity/fuel (Fig. 6.2).

As far as the net profit/loss scenario before and after privatization is concerned, we can notice that the company has been sustaining net losses even after privatization in 2005 (Ahmed & Bhatti (2019), Bacon (2019)).

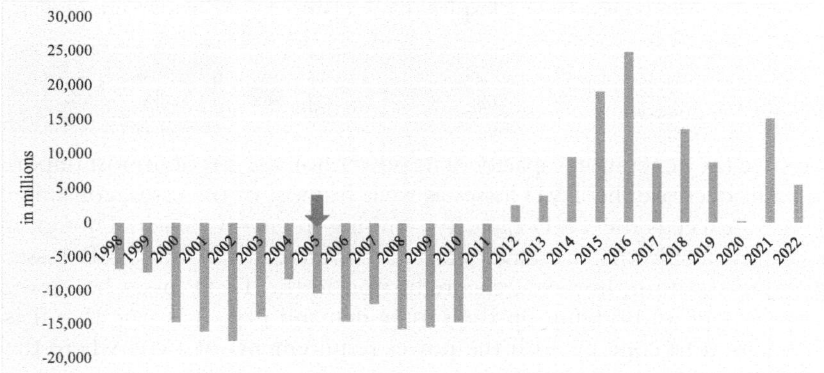

Fig. 6.2 Net Profit/loss of K-electric. (*Source*: Based on data taken from Annual Reports of K-Electric, 2007–2022)

KE observed its first profit only in 2012 after several years of consistent losses but the profit declined again in 2020. Though during all these years, the company had been receiving hefty amount of receivables under the head of tariff adjustment as a result of a rise in the fuel cost. The highest amount of tariff adjustment had been received in 2022 (172687 million PKR). The drastic fall in net profits in 2020 has been attributed by the company officials to the macroeconomic factors, trickled down through various channels. These include surge in inflation, increase in policy rates, and a decrease in economic activity due to COVID-19.

Transmission and Distribution Losses

Earlier it was discussed that KE performed poorly in improving its generation capacity to meet the power demand coming from the consumers, which was mainly attributed to the unavailability of fuel. Another reason behind the long and persistent load shedding in the nation's largest city and the center of its commercial life has been the transmission and distribution losses. T&D losses occur due to technical and commercial reasons. Technical losses are inherent in every system and are caused by energy that is lost. Through the use of technology, these can be minimized to the best possible extent. However, theft or illegal absorption of power is the main cause of commercial losses. Despite many claims by KE's management to

improve the generation capacity of its power houses, it is of utmost importance to decrease the T&D losses as well. In most of the cases, consumer demand exceeds the T&D capacity resulting in energy deficit. Though it is commendable that we have seen a 55% reduction in the T&D losses after privatization, however, this reduction in the T&D losses has never been enough in bridging up the supply-demand gap. It is true that it is challenging to cope up with the power requirements of a city where the population witnesses a mushroom growth, where the law and order situation is adverse, and where the legal procedures are cumbersome, however, there is always a way when there is a will (Fig. 6.3).

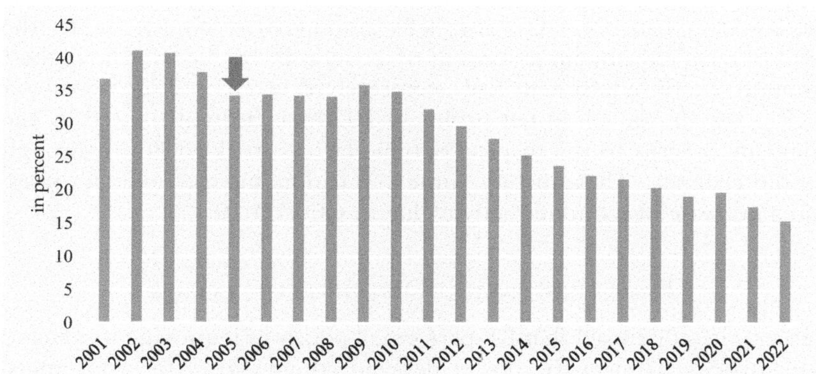

Fig. 6.3 Transmission and distribution losses. (*Source*: Based on data taken from annual of K-Electric, 2007–2002)

Tariff Adjustment Subsidy

As per the definition in the annual reports of KE, tariff differential subsidy is claimed by KE from the government when there is a sudden change in the fuel prices, cost of power, maintenance and operation cost, write-offs of trade debts and unrecovered cost (Fig. 6.4).

This tariff adjustment is usually carried on a quarterly basis. Before 2005, there was a limit of 4% variation in cost which was to be covered by tariff subsidy. The remaining burden was supposed to be carried forward to the next quarter. However, adverse movements in the fuel prices since 2005 caused additional burden on the company which could not be recovered and is categorized under "unrecovered cost." Except for the years from 2014 to 2017, we can notice a constant rise in the tariff differential subsidy. It has skyrocketed in 2022 which is expected to be increasing in the coming years. For the government it has become a fiscal sustainability issue. There is a dire need of reliable, affordable, and indigenous sources of energy. The cost of imported fuel is always tied to the prices in the international markets; hence, the cost of power production becomes huge resulting in persistent fiscal burden as well as continuous power deficit.

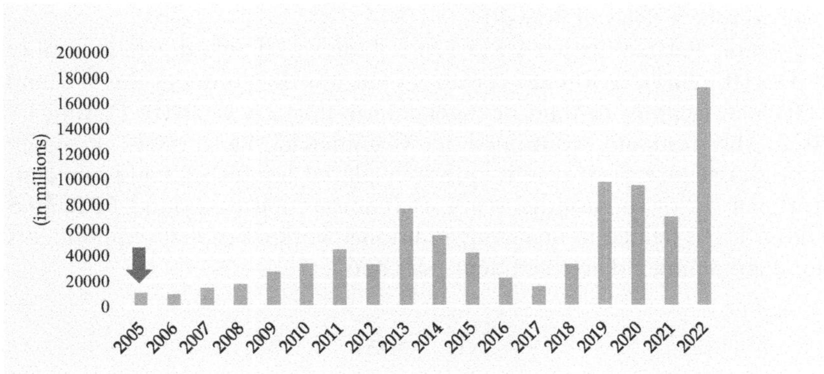

Fig. 6.4 Tariff adjustment subsidy. (*Source*: Based on data taken from Annual Reports of K-Electric, 2007–2022)

Investments Scenario after Privatization

Since Privatization KE has invested US$ 4.1 billion across the power value chain, added 1507 MW to installed generation capacity, and reduced 18.9% of T&D losses (Annual Report, 2022). It demonstrated a resolute commitment to fortifying its infrastructure and operations through strategic investments. Substantial capital expenditure had been earmarked for the expansion of internal generation, rehabilitation of the existing transmission and distribution network, and improvement in overall business operations and customer services.

In this regard, KESC entered into loan agreements in 2007 with International Finance Corporation (IFC) and Asian Development Bank (ADB) in order to avail long-term financing of up to USD 275 million to finance the Korangi 220 MW and 560 MW BQPS power plants. It is pertinent to point out that these power plants had been the first addition to generation capacity after 1997. Extensive engagements with IFC and ADB were necessary during that year to ensure that committed loans remained available as significant changes in the country's environment and international financing markets had made international lenders much more cautious. After exhaustive negotiations, IFC and ADB agreed to maintain the loan commitments signed in 2007 and to restructure the loans to reflect delayed drawdown.

In June 2010, a further USD 115 million was drawn down. A total of USD 210 million of foreign currency debt was drawn under the IFC and ADB loan facilities to fund new generation projects in 2010. During FY 2022, the company continued its Commercial Paper (CP) Program through issuance of six distinct privately placed Islamic CPs and one conventional CP of six months' tenor each amounting to around PKR 30.5 billion. It has helped in financing additional working capital requirements and maintaining a diversified debt portfolio.

KE Today

Challenging sociopolitical and macroeconomic factors have had a cascading impact on multiple sectors including KE. Surging inflation, policy rate hike, and reduction in economic activity had a significant impact on the company's operations and profitability. Impacted by these challenges, the company has observed a reduction in units sent-out by 5.8% and the gross profitability of the company declined significantly by PKR 7.0 billion (KE Quarterly Report, 2023).

Further, the company faced an increase in exchange loss by PKR 8.6 billion owing to significant devaluation of Pak Rupee and increase in impairment loss by PKR 9.8 billion against doubtful debts due to high inflation, increase in consumer tariff and deteriorating economic conditions impacting consumer propensity to pay. The aforementioned factors along with drastic increase in finance cost by PKR 11.8 billion mainly on account of increase in effective rate of borrowing and higher levels of borrowing due to non-payment of dues by government entities, translated into the loss after tax amounting to PKR 39.4 billion.

Concluding Remarks

The success/failure status of KE after privatization was discussed on the basis of four pillars—generation capacity, T&D losses, net profit/loss scenario, and the fiscal burden it lays on the government treasury. We noticed that there isn't any significant increase in the generation capacity of KE over a period of 17 years. The net profit/loss scenario is also not much satisfying. The company experienced its first net profit only in 2012. However, after 2016 the profit started to decrease again. The T&D losses also experienced a declining trend after privatization but this decline was not sufficient to cover the power deficit of the city. Resultantly, the company, being a private company has proved to remain a burden on the government machinery. In view of all this, we have come to the consensus that KE is an ineffective electric utility. Particularly in summers, when power demand rises, KE's performance is heavily criticized.

Box 6.5 Electricity Supply Chain

There are several moving parts to the supply chain. After power is generated in powerhouses, the voltage is stepped up to be transmitted via primary transmission lines to 500/220 kilovolt grid stations. In these grid stations, the voltage is converted to 132 kv and then transmitted via secondary transmission lines to 132 kv grid stations. From here, they are transmitted to distribution lines and delivered to consumers. The capacity of all these units—primary transmission lines, secondary transmission lines, grid stations, distribution lines, distribution transformers—has failed to keep pace with the increase in generation capacity.

(*continued*)

(continued)

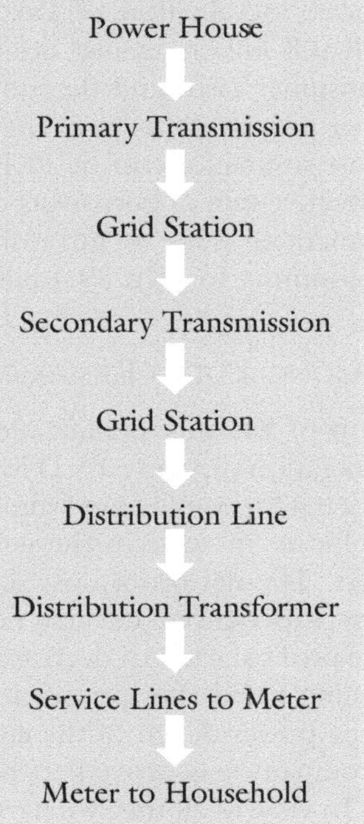

References

Ahmed, T., & Bhatti, A. A. (2019). Do power sector reforms affect electricity prices in selected Asian countries? *Energy Policy, 129*, 1253–1260.

Bacon, R. (2019). Learning from power sector reform: The case of Pakistan. *World Bank policy research working paper*, (8842).

Dad, M. (2021). The effect of privatization on the performance of employees a case study on Karachi Electric Supply Company. *International Journal of Experiential Learning & Case Studies, 6*(2), 97–119.

Jamil, M. H., Ullah, K., Saleem, N., Abbas, F., & Khalid, H. A. (2022). Did the restructuring of the electricity generation sector increase social welfare in Pakistan? *Renewable and Sustainable Energy Reviews, 157*, 112017.

Qazi, U., & Jahanzaib, M. (2018). An integrated sectoral framework for the development of sustainable power sector in Pakistan. *Energy Reports, 4*, 376–392.

Tiep, N. C., Wang, M., Mohsin, M., Kamran, H. W., & Yazdi, F. A. (2021). An assessment of power sector reforms and utility performance to strengthen consumer self-confidence towards private investment. *Economic Analysis and Policy, 69*, 676–689.

Ullah, K., Arentsen, M. J., & Lovett, J. C. (2017). Institutional determinants of power sector reform in Pakistan. *Energy Policy, 102*, 332–339.

CHAPTER 7

Cement Industry Case Study

Abstract The history of Pakistan's cement industry dates back to 1921, with the establishment of the first plant in Wah. Following nationalization in 1972, the State Cement Corporation of Pakistan (SCCP) observed significant growth in production capacity. However, the industry underwent privatization starting in 1991, transitioning into private ownership. This chapter provides a comprehensive overview of the cement industry in Pakistan, focusing on the key players like Maple Leaf Cement, Kohat Cement, and D.G. Cement. It examines their pre- and post-privatization performance, highlighting challenges and opportunities. Despite facing hurdles, such as payment issues and legal battles during privatization, these companies attracted buyers and underwent significant changes in ownership. Post-privatization, they experienced fluctuations in profitability influenced by factors like production costs, currency depreciation, and market dynamics.

Keywords Pakistan's Cement Industry • Maple Leaf Cement • Kohat Cement • D.G. Cement • Market Dynamics of Cement Industry

Cement production is amongst one of the thriving businesses in Pakistan, contributing most to the federal budget in terms of taxes. According to Pakistan's economic survey for FY 2021–2022, the GDP contribution of

G. Samad, N. Faraz, *The Face of Privatization in Pakistan*,
https://doi.org/10.1007/978-981-97-8385-4_7

the construction sector is 2.56%. However, according to data from the All Pakistan Cement Manufacturers Association (APCMA), the exports of cement had the biggest fall in FY2022, which is mostly attributable to global inflation and unfavorable prices. This chapter will look into the history of the cement industry and its performance before and after its privatization.

History of Cement Industry

The beginning of Pakistan's cement industry started with the establishment of its first plant at Wah in 1921. At the time of independence in 1947, there were a total of four cement industries situated at Wah, Dandot, Rohri, and Karachi, with an installed capacity of 470,000 tons annually. Two facilities were developed by the Pakistan Industrial Development Corporation (PIDC) in 1956 in Daudkel and Hyderabad, and more units were later built by the private sector.

Following the Economic Reforms Order of 1972, the industry was nationalized, and the State Cement Corporation of Pakistan (SCCP) was created. As a result, public cement units in Pakistan were managed by SCCP. Following nationalization, the SCCP received ownership of a total of ten cement manufacturing facilities with an installed capacity of 2.8 million tons annually. The SCCP developed five additional facilities with an installed capacity of 1.8 million tons annually while the cement sector was operating under state control. During 1987–1988, the public sector firms accounted for 81.3% of total cement production. We can observe some interesting facts on the financial position of the cement industry in the public sector. The rate of return on equity has been increasing overtime from 23.3% in 1983–1984 to 52% in 1987–1988. The same is the case of rate of return on total and fixed assets which became doubled in 1987–1988 from what it was in 1983–1984. This shows that the public sector firms in the cement industry came out to be the winners in the given indicators of performance (Tables 7.1 and 7.2).

Table 7.1 Financial position of SCCP during 1987–1988

Number of Firms	14
Number of Loss-making Firm	3
Net income (excluding financial charges)	1056
Net income (including financial charges)	1312
Net Equity	2032

Source: Naqvi and Kemal (1991)

Table 7.2 Pre-privatization performance of SCCP

	1983–84	*1984–85*	*1985–86*	*1986–87*	*1987–88*
Rate of Return on Equity	23.3	32.7	47.8	53.5	52.0
Rate of Return on total Assets	9.4	12.1	14.9	17.9	17.9
Rate of Return on fixed Assets	13.7	16.7	21. 1	26.8	27.9

Source: Naqvi and Kemal (1991)

The Process of Privatization

The deregulation of the cement business started in 1985–1986 when the private sector was allowed to establish cement facilities as well. However, by that time, the SCCP had an absolute control over price fixing and was in charge of the majority of the capacity. The private sector built more factories as a result of severe scarcity of cement and price deregulation. After the termination of the state monopoly, the first cement plant in the private sector to launch commercial operations was Cherat Cement (1985) by Ghulam Fauque Group. Upper Punjab and KP are its two primary marketplaces. The privatization process of the public units actually started in 1991, before that, seven units were already established in the private sector. During the Nawaz regime in 1992, government privatized eight cement companies including Maple Leaf Cement, Pak Cement, White Cement, D.G. Khan Cement, Dandot Cement, Gharibwal Cement, Zeal Pak Cement and Kohat Cement. Out of the cement businesses that the Nawaz Sharif administration privatized, D.G. Khan Cement was the most valued and enjoyed monopoly in its region. It was the most up-to-date facility of all those owned by the SCCP, with the majority of the depreciation amortized and the interest payments paid. By the end of its first fiscal year following privatization, Dandot Cement, which had been deregulated in 1992, was able to eliminate all of its prior losses. Through an optimization program that was concluded in July 1995, it has boosted its daily capacity from 1000 tons to 1600 tons. On the down side, Dandot had a troubled labor-management relationship that previously resulted in plant closure and was a heavily unionized company. As a result of the much-discussed Dhan Fibers project's delayed start, investors were also beginning to lose faith in the group. Javedan Cement Company Limited ceased its operation in cement manufacturing after being privatized and is involved in the housing schemes now. It is now named as Javedan Corporation Limited.

The privatization process of some of the companies discussed above was completed in 1992, but for some it delayed due to payment issues and court cases, and thus was completed in 1996. National Cement was privatized in 1995, while General Refractories Limited and Wah Cement were privatized in 1996. The Musharraf regime sold out the remaining cement manufacturing units till 2006. Since then, the cement industry is being operated by the private investors (Table 7.3).

Table 7.3 Privatization of public cement units

Company	*Sale Price (in Million rupees)*	*Date of transfer*	*Buyer's name*
Maple Leaf Cement	486	January 1992	Nishat Mills Ltd.
Pak Cement	189	January 1992	Mian Jahangir Ellahi & Associates
White Cement	138	January 1992	Mian Jahangir Ellahi & Associates
D.G Khan Cement	1961	May 1992	Tariq Sehgal & Associates
Dandot Cement	637	May 1992	EMG
Garibwal Cement	836	September 1992	Haji Saifullah & Group
Zeal Pak Cement	240	October 1992	Sardar M. Ashraf D. Baluch
Kohat Cement	528	October 1992	Palace Enterprises
Dandot Works-National Cement	110	January 1995	EMG
General Refractories Limited	19	February 1996	Shah Rukh Engineering
Wah Cement	2416	February 1996	EMG
Associated Cement Rohri	255	November 2003	National Transport Khi
Thatta Cement	794	January 2004	Al Abbass Group
Dandot Cement (10% additional sahres)	8	October 2004	EMG
Kohat Cement (10% additional shares)	41	October 2004	EMG
Mustehkam Cement Limited	3205	November 2005	Bestway Cement Limited
Javedan Cement Company Limited	4316	August 2006	Haji Ghani Usman & Group

Source: Privatization Commission of Pakistan

a. **Maple Leaf Cement Limited**

MLCFL was established in 1956 by the West Pakistan Industrial Development Corporation (WPIDC) and incorporated as "Maple Leaf Cement Factory Limited (MLCFL)." The capacity of the plant was 300,000 tons clinker per annum. A subsidiary of the MLCFL by the name of White Cement Industries Limited (WCIL) was established in 1967 with a capacity of 15,000 tons per annum. In 1974, the management was transferred to SCCP as part of nationalization policy in the country. In 1983, SCCP expanded WCIL's white cement plant by adding another unit of the same capacity parallel to the existing one; it increased total capacity to 30,000 tons clinker per annum. In 1986, SCCP set up another production unit of gray cement under the name of Pak Cement Company Limited (PCCL) with a capacity of 180,000 tons per annum. In 1992, MLCFL, WCIL, and PCCL were privatized and transferred to the Kohinoor Mills Limited Group (KMLG). All three companies were merged into Maple Leaf Cement Factory Limited on July 1, 1992.

Pre-Privatization Performance of Maple Leaf Cement

The statistics in Table 7.4 shows that MLFCL was performing quite well before its privatization. The RoR on net equity showed an increase of 600% in 1987–1988 of what it was in 1983–1984. The rate of increase in RoR on paid-up capital was even more than that. In short, it was performing well when it was under state control.

After Privatization Performance of MLCF

In order to analyze the post-privatization performance of MLCF, we had to rely on the data from the annual reports of MLCF which are available since 2007 only. It would have been better if we could have data on the performance of the company in early 1990s when it was just privatized. We would have been in a better position to analyze the position of the company right before privatization (Fig. 7.1).

According to the information that was accessible, the corporation after privatization only started making a profit in 2012 after years of significant losses. However, profit margins decreased once more in FY 2018 as a

Table 7.4 Pre-privatization Financial Status of Maple Leaf Cement

	1983–1984	*1984–1985*	*1985–1986*	*1986–1987*	*1987–1988*
RoR on Net Equity	22.7	178.0	180.5	179.4	160.2
RoR on Paid-up Capital	28.3	229.4	276.3	302.6	337.0
RoR on Fixed Assets	21.2	137.9	146.8	129.0	150.1
RoR on Total Assets	6.6	38.9	50.0	53.5	55.2
Mark-up on Sales	5.6	28.2	30.4	31.3	26.8

Source: Naqvi and Kemal (1991)

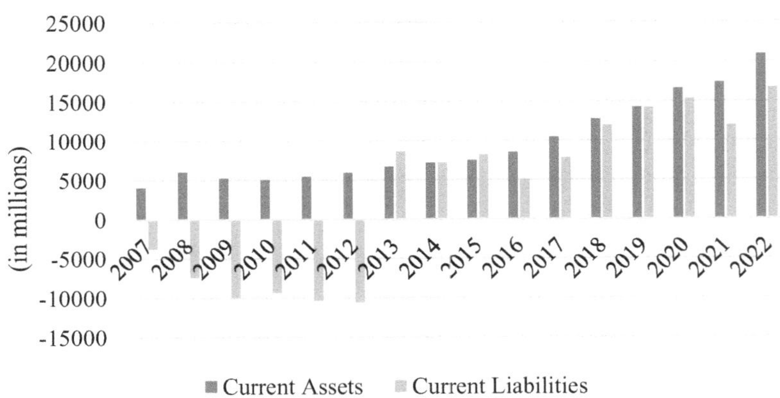

Fig. 7.1 Current Assets and Liabilities of MLCF. (*Source*: Annual Reports of MLCF, 2012–2022)

result of a high cost of production brought on by an upsurge in coal rates and power expenses. The cost of production also increased in FY 2019 principally as a result of higher input prices caused by the depreciation of the Pakistani rupee. Input prices continued to rise in FY 2020, which resulted in losses as sales retention dropped and costs of sales rose. In comparison to sales of 13,073 million PKR in 2011, the company's net sales in 2012 increased by 18% to 15,461 million PKR. Improved manufacturing and decreased overhead expenses led to higher retention rates, which in turn led to an increase in sales. Due to ongoing reconstruction activities, export sales to Afghanistan increased. Heavy gas and electricity load shedding in 2011–2012 made the energy crisis worse and had a negative impact on production costs. Production costs were increased by high Fuel Price Adjustment fees (FPA) in energy tariffs (Fig. 7.2).

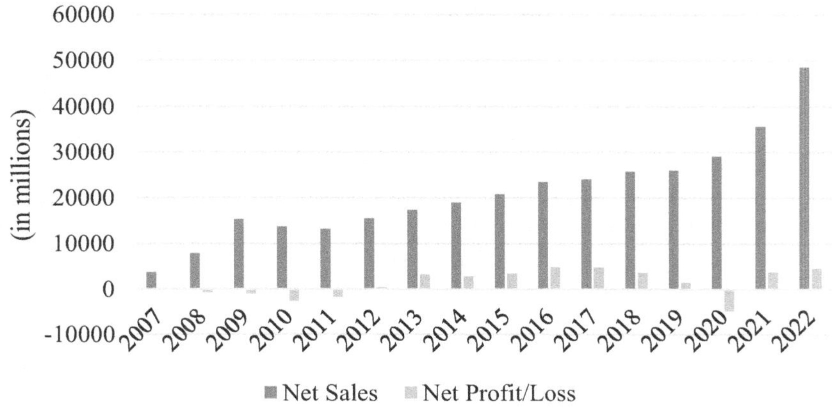

Fig. 7.2 Net Sales and Net Profits/Loss of MLCF. (*Source*: Annual Reports of MLCF, 2012–2022)

Current assets showed an increasing trend from 2007 to 2022; however, current liabilities also showed an increasing trend after 2012.

Post-Privatization Investment Scenario of MLCF

The company was first listed on all Stock Exchanges in Pakistan in 1994. In 1998, a separate production line for gray Portland cement of 990,000 tons per annum clinker capacity based on most modern dry process technology was installed.

In 2000, Maple Leaf Electric Company Limited (MLEC), a power generation unit, was merged into the company. In 2004, the coal conversion project at new dry process plant was completed. In 2005, dry process plant capacity was increased from 3300 tpd to 4000 tpd through debottlenecking and up-gradation of equipment and necessary adjustments in operational parameters.

In 2006, a project to convert the existing wet process line to a fuel-efficient dry process white cement line commenced its commercial production. In 2007, the company undertook another expansion project of 6700 tpd gray clinker capacity which commenced its commercial production on November 1, 2007. In 2008, two existing lines of white cement 50 tpd each clinker capacity converted into oil well cement plant which started its commercial production. In 2011, the company successfully started Waste Heat Recovery Boiler Plant. In 2012, it started earning profit and recorded PKR 496 million profit after tax. In 2013, it earned the highest ever record profit after tax of PKR 3225 million. In 2014, the company and Pakistan Railway signed an agreement to transport coal and cement from Karachi to Daudkhel and vice versa. This whole scenario shows that MLCF has been on the track of success after privatization in terms of its engagements in new projects.

b. **Kohat Cement**

Kohat Cement was established in 1983 under SCCP with an annual capacity of 300,000 tons. It was privatized in an open bidding by the Government of Pakistan in 1992. Under the new management, the capacity of the plant was enhanced with the collaboration of a German company. The company was registered on the stock exchanges of Pakistan in 1994, while entered into the global market in 2002.

Pre-Privatization Performance of Kohat Cement

The pre-privatization performance of Kohat Cement shows that apart from a negative rate of return on net equity and paid-up capital during 1984–1985 and 1985–1986, overall the company was performing well before privatization (Table 7.5).

Table 7.5 Pre-privatization Financials of Kohat Cement

	1983–1984	*1984–1985*	*1985–1986*	*19871988*	*1988–1989*
RoR on Net Equity	2.6	Negative	Negative	17.9	20.6
RoR on Paid up Capital	2.7	Negative	Negative	24.8	33.3
RoR on fixed Assets	6.0	0.7	5.1	11.1	11.8

Source: Naqvi and Kemal (1991)

Post-Privatization Performance of Kohat Cement

Though the pre-privatization performance of Kohat Cement was decent, it did quite well after privatization as well. We have analyzed some of the performance indicators below.

Net Sales

Net sales showed an increasing trend since 2003 except for the year 2020, where it experienced a dip. For the economies of the world and Pakistan, 2020 was a year unlike any other. After 68 years, the national economy saw negative GDP growth as a result of the lockdowns implemented to curb the spread of COVID-19. The nation's cement industry saw a negligible growth of 1.98%. The commissioning of new cement lines with a capacity of 9 million tons together with the low growth in cement demand for the year both resulted in a 14% decrease in plant capacity utilization of the company. This led to a downward spiral in cement pricing on the domestic market and a 28% decline in sales revenue for Kohat Cement, which resulted in losses for the company (Fig. 7.3).

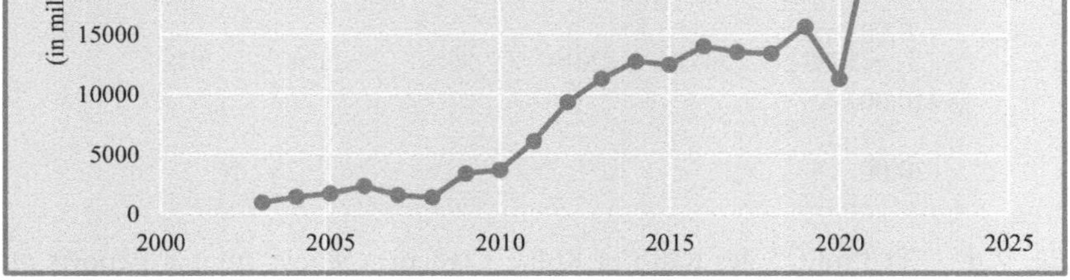

Fig. 7.3 Net Sales of Kohat Cement. (*Source*: Annual Reports of Kohat Cement, 2009–2022)

Net Profit/Loss

As far as the data on net profit/loss is concerned, we can see that the company's profitability scenario had not been satisfying till 2011. It had either been experiencing losses or a small amount of profit compared to the years following 2011. The years it had been experiencing losses were 2008, 2010, and 2020. It should be noted that Kohat Cement is located near Indus Highway, on the southern side of Kohat Tunnel while darra Adam Khel is located on the northern side. This whole area was inflicted by "War on Terror" due to which company's operation suffered badly. In particular, the irregular power supply because of blowing up of main power transmission lines by militants and frequent closure of Kohat tunnel due to Army operations in Darra against militants resulted in the loss of production and sales. The year 2009 was when there was a low domestic demand for cement, while during 2010, the export market remained under pressure for the cement industry. As a result, during the loss years, the company was unable to meet its debt obligations and acquired deferment facility on principal payments for one year (Fig. 7.4 and 7.5).

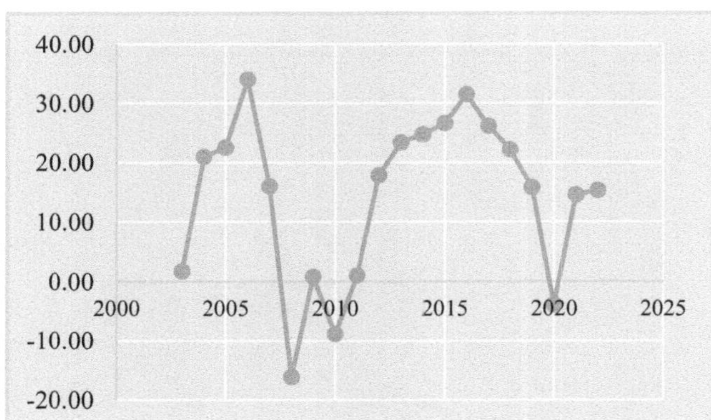

Fig. 7.4 Net Profit/Sales Ratio of Kohat Cement. (*Source*: Annual Reports of Kohat Cement, 2009–2022)

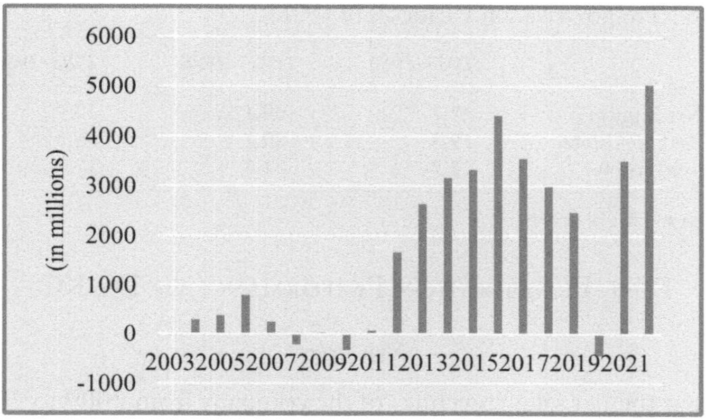

Fig. 7.5 Net Profit/Loss of Kohat Cement. (*Source*: Annual Reports of Kohat Cement, 2009–2022)

c. **D.G. Cement Company Limited**

D.G. Cement was established in 1978 under SCCP and entered into commercial production in 1986. The company had primarily been involved in the manufacturing and sale of clinker, ordinary Portland, and sulphate-resistant cement. It has four cement facilities, two of which are in Dera Ghazi Khan, one in the Hub District of Lasbela, and one in the Khairpur District of Chakwal. In 1992, it was acquired by Nishat Group under the privatization program of the government. It kept on increasing its existing production capacity as well as installing new production plants in the subsequent years. As of now, it is the third largest manufacturer of cement in Pakistan. It is the only company whose production facilities span the entire country from North to South having a wide-ranging dealer network. In order to compare the pre- and post-privatization performance of DGKC, let us have a look at the following statistics.

Pre-Privatization Performance of DGKC

The pre-privatization financial ratios of DGKC show that the rate of return on net equity showed a huge increase from 1985–1986 to 1988–1989. The same has been the case with the rate of return on paid up capital and fixed assets (Table 7.6).

Table 7.6 Pre-privatization Financials of DGKC

	1985–1986	*1987–1988*	*1988–1989*
RoR on Net Equity	2.2	29.1	32.9
RoR on Paid up Capital	19.8	30.7	36.3
RoR on fixed Assets	2.2	22.3	27.7

Source: Naqvi and Kemal (1991)

Post-Privatization Performance of DGKC

Net Sales

Looking at the net sales (revenue) of the company from 2009 to 2022, an increasing trend can be observed in the net sales of the company during the whole period. However, two slight declines can also be seen: one in 2010 (a decrease of 9.77%) and the other in 2020 (4.7% decline). The earlier fall was mostly brought on by reduced selling prices on the global market as well as fierce competition among cement producers that resulted in price wars. This fall in the sales revenue was not due to a fall in the local dispatches (which actually increased by 45%) but due to a fall of 20% in export sales, mainly to India. The latter decline was mainly due to the impact of COVID-19. Some other reasons included a falling cement price, rising costs mainly due to the withdrawal of PM Relief, and currency devaluation. Moreover, exports of cement declined mainly due to a halt of exports to India after imposition of 200% duty (Fig. 7.6).

Net Profit/Loss

Net profit/loss situation of DGKC shows that the company has been experiencing a net profit situation throughout the period under study except for the year 2020 due to COVID-19 pandemic. However, the overall profits declined after 2018. With slow demand, price war, and an unfavorable export market affecting the sales side and rising production costs due to general inflation, utility price increase, the devaluation of the rupee, and interest rate hikes affecting the cost side, the company performed poorly in the fiscal year 2019. There was a slight decline in the profits in 2017 as well which was attributed to an increase in the federal excise duty by the government. Second, the local net selling price also declined during this period which put a negative impact on the profitability of the company (Fig. 7.7).

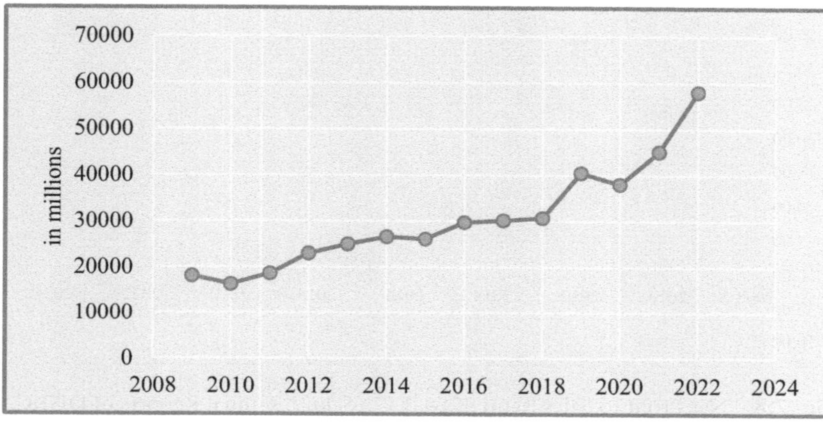

Fig. 7.6 Net Sales of DGKC. (*Source*: Annual Reports of DGKC, 2014–2022)

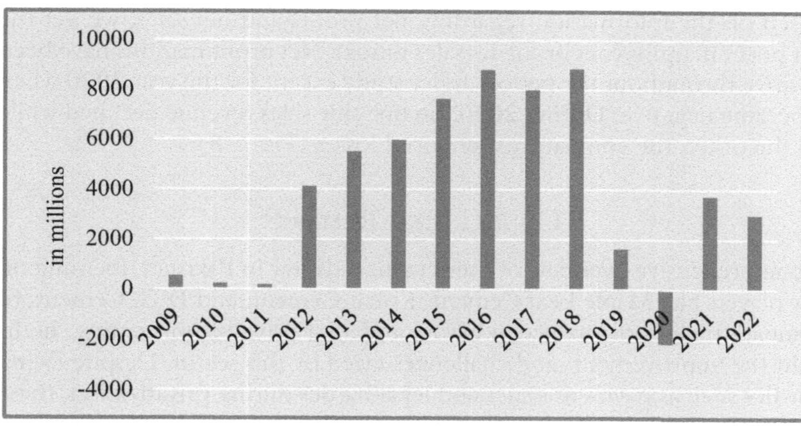

Fig. 7.7 Net Profit/Loss of DGKC. (*Source*: Annual Reports of DGKC, 2014–2022)

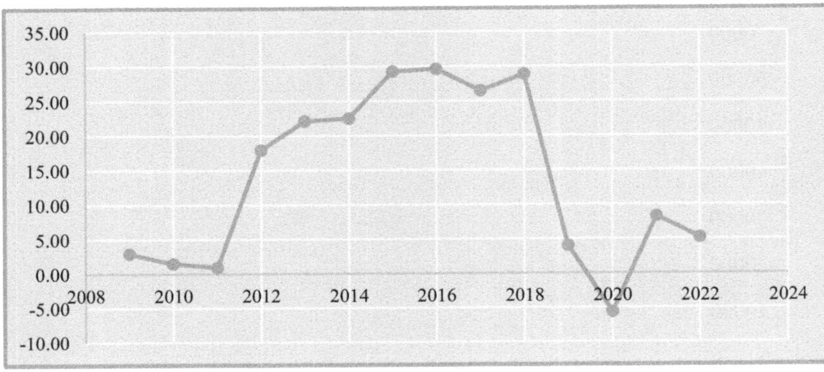

Fig. 7.8 Net Profit to Sales Ratio of DGKC. (*Source*: Annual Reports of DGKC, 2014–2022)

Net Profit to Sales Ratio

Based on the information regarding net profits and net sales, we get the net profit margins (net profit-to-sales ratios). Net profit margins have been positive throughout the period under study except for the year 2020 when it became negative. During 2020, on one side sales revenue declined while on the other, the company experienced losses (Fig. 7.8).

Concluding Remarks

A comprehensive overview of the cement industry in Pakistan, focusing on key players like Maple Leaf Cement, Kohat Cement, and D.G. Cement, to compare their performance in before and after privatization setting, highlight the improvements and challenges faced by this sector. Despite facing hurdles such as payment issues and legal battles during privatization, these major companies of this sector attracted buyers and underwent significant ownership changes. In post-privatization period, they experienced fluctuations in performance which is influenced by factors like production costs, currency depreciation, and market dynamics.

Reference

Naqvi, S. N. H., & Kemal, A. R. (1991). The privatization of the public industrial enterprises in Pakistan. *The Pakistan Development Review*, 105–144.

CHAPTER 8

Telecom Sector: Case Study of Pakistan Telecommunication Company Limited (PTCL)

Abstract Pakistan Telecommunication Company (PTCL) serving as a pivotal entity in the nation's telecom sector underwent significant shifts in its financial dynamics following its privatization in 2006. Chapter 8 provides an in-depth exploration of the privatization and subsequent performance of PTCL. Before privatization, PTCL demonstrated robust financial metrics, making substantial contributions to the national treasury. However, post-privatization, the company encountered challenges, experiencing declines in operating profit, net income, and return on equity. Despite a sudden revenue surge in 2020 attributed to increased demand for broadband services amid digitalization trends, PTCL's net profit stagnated, exacerbated by high-debt ratios resulting from leverage.

This chapter critically evaluates the efficacy of the privatization decision, shedding light on transparency concerns raised by discrepancies in property transfers and the sale of shares to a foreign investor. Ultimately, the analysis underscores the paramount importance of transparency and welfare considerations in privatization endeavors, advocating for a balanced approach to safeguard the long-term success of national assets.

Keywords Pakistan Telecommunication Company (PTCL) • Telecom Sector in Pakistan • Privatization of PTCL in 2006 • Financial Dynamics of PTCL • Balanced Approach in Privatization

G. Samad, N. Faraz, *The Face of Privatization in Pakistan*,
https://doi.org/10.1007/978-981-97-8385-4_8

PTCL, the only national telecommunication company being privatized, serves as the backbone of the country's telecommunication infrastructure despite the influx of many other telecom operators. Originally an SOE, the shareholding of PTCL by the government was reduced to 62%, when 26% of shares and management control were handed over to a UAE-based company—Etisilat International Pakistan (EIP)—in 2006. Rest of 12% of the shares had already been offered to the general public in 1994 under an intensified privatization program.

The rationale behind the privatization of PTCL was that it was considered to be an inefficient, unproductive and outdated business giant that was impeding the progress of telecommunication sector in Pakistan. However, the general consensus has been that PTCL was a leading telecommunication company in Asia before being privatized. On one side, it employed a sizeable group of highly qualified technicians, and on the other, its financial success was also remarkable. Let us have a look on some of the statistics regarding the financial performance of PTCL before and after privatization.

Pre-Privatization Performance of PTCL

Four years before privatization, there was an increase of 11% per annum in the net profits of the company from around 18 billion to over 27 billion PKR. In 2005, a year before its privatization, PTCL posted revenues of 84 billion rupees, with earnings before interest, tax, and depreciation of 54 billion PKR and a net profit of 27 billion PKR. It earned 5.72 PKR per share in the fiscal year 2004. In the same year, it had a 35.7% return on equity. Most importantly, its contribution to national exchequer was huge. Its contribution in the form of GST and withholding tax was 9.5 billion PKR, while in the form of corporate income tax and dividends, it contributed 16.2 billion and 15.7 billion PKR, respectively. Its entire financial contribution to the government coffers was, therefore, 41.4 billion PKR.

Post-privatization Performance of PTCL

The situation after privatization seemed to have been deteriorated as demonstrated in Table 8.1.

It can be seen that the operating profit of the PTCL declined from 39.4% in 2006 to 21% in 2011. As far the net income is concerned, it was 26.2% in 2006 which decreased to 13.5 in 2011. Return on Equity (ROE)

Table 8.1 Post-privatization Operating Profit of PTCL

Year	*2006*	*2007*	*2008*	*2009*	*2010*	*2011*
Operating profit %	39.4	34. 1	(5.4)	25.2	25.7	21
Net Income RS (%)	26.2	22.0	(4.3)	15.4	16.3	13.5
ROE	20.22	14.45	(2.71)	9.28	9.33	7.50

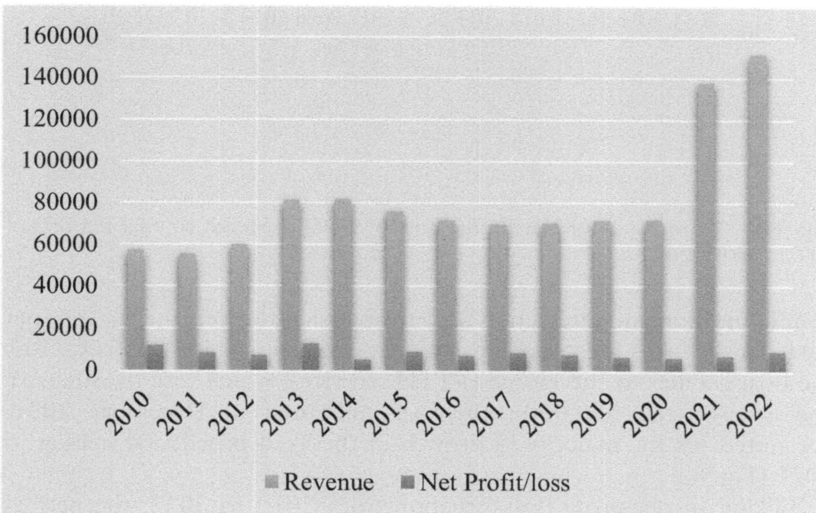

Fig. 8.1 Post privatization performance of PTCL

was 20.22% right after privatization in 2006, which decreased and recorded a negative value in 2008. Later, it increased again but remained lower than what it was in 2006 (Figs. 8.1 and 8.2).

Considering the data from the annual financial statements of PTCL from 2010 to 2022, we have observed that the revenue growth has been fluctuating and remained low till 2020. However, surprisingly, in 2021 and 2022, a sudden jump in the growth rate of revenue could be observed. This was mainly driven by growth in broadband sales and corporate and wholesale business segments. Furthermore, due to new working arrangements like work from home, e-learning, and digitalization, the shift in

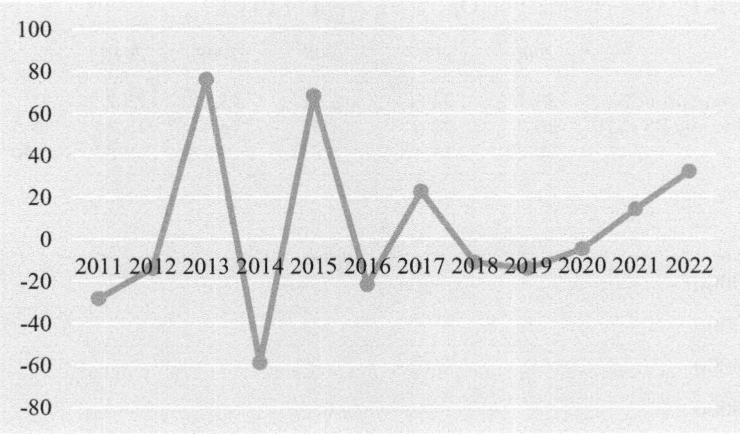

Fig. 8.2 Growth rate of Net Profit/Loss of PTCL. (*Source*: Annual Reports of PTCL, 2013–2021)

communication and interaction patterns boosted the demand for internet data. This led to a greater reliance on data and connection services across the board. Fiber to the Home (FTTH) services, which rose by 30% YoY and crossed the 580,000 subscriber milestone in December 2021, accounted for the majority of growth in the fixed broadband market in 2021 (Fig. 8.3).

Talking of net profit/loss situation from 2010 to 2022, the performance seemed to be unsatisfactory since the annual growth in the net profits continued to remain stagnant throughout the period under consideration. An increasing trend in the growth rate of net profit/loss could be observed after 2019 but before that the growth did not show any stability.

The lower growth in the net profits had been attributed to the high debt ratios of the company which remained more than 40% from 2013 to 2021. This clearly indicates that PTCL, despite being the backbone of telecommunication in the country, remained a highly leveraged company after privatization Ansar et al. (2013), Asghar et al. (2016), Choudhary & Asghar (2016), Haroon-Ur-Rashid et al. (2009).

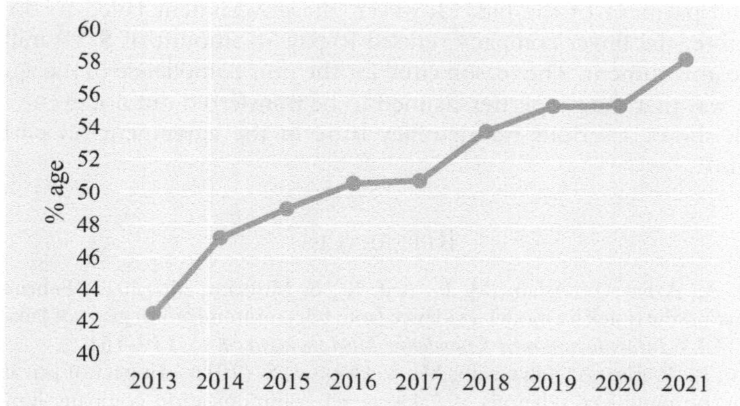

Fig. 8.3 Debt ratios of PTCL. (*Source*: Annual Reports of PTCL, 2013–2021)

Privatization of PTCL: Welfare and Transparency

From the financial position of the company discussed above, we come to the conclusion that PTCL should not have been privatized at first place. It was performing quite well being a state-owned enterprise. However, if the government somehow decided to privatize this national asset, it should have taken into consideration some of the important aspects related to it. The most important amongst all has been the welfare of the country. However, it is evident that the privatization decision did not take into account the welfare aspect. The sale of the 26% company shares were transferred to a foreign company. According to Pakistan's own experience, privatization through the sale of shares to the general population is far more focused on welfare and success than privatization through the sale of shares to international investors Haroon-Ur-Rashid et al. (2009), Ibrar et al. (2015), Malik et al. (2011), Siddiqi et al. (2012), Siddiqui & Mangi (2013). The sale to a foreign investor has an ongoing negative impact on the balance of payments position of the country. No nation has ever benefited from economic progress by selling valuable public enterprises to foreign investors.

The second most import aspect is the transparency in the agreement between the two parties. According to the privatization agreement, the Government of Pakistan had to transfer 3384 properties of PTCL to Etisilat International, after which the UAE-based company had to transfer the full payment of the bid. However, the government failed to do so, therefore, the buyer company refused to pay an amount of $799 million to the government. The reason cited for the non-compliance of the agreement was that the properties claimed to be transferred did not even exist, which shows a serious transparency issue in the agreement on part of the GoP.

References

Ansar, A., Azhar, T., Aslam, M. F., Arif, K., & Mubeen, M. (2013, February). Beyond the quick fix model–evidence from telecommunication giant of Pakistan 'PTCL'. *Information and Knowledge Management, 4*(4), 139–151.

Asghar, B., Wasim, A., Jahanzaib, M., & Hussain, S. (2016). Impact of privatization on employee relations at Pakistan telecommunication company limited. *The Nucleus, 53*(4), 243–253.

Choudhary, M. A., & Asghar, B. (2016, September). Post-privatization reorientation of employee relations: A case study of Pakistan Telecommunication Company Limited (PTCL). In *In 2016 Portland International conference on Management of Engineering and Technology (PICMET)* (pp. 2351–2362). IEEE.

Haroon-Ur-Rashid, H., Shah, M. A. J., Ullah, H., & Ahmed, S. (2009). Impact of privatization: 'Managing the process of privatization and its impacts on performance and development: A case study of Pakistan Telecommunication Limited'.

Ibrar, M., Shafique, M. N., Ahmad, N., & Abbas, H. (2015). Pay and job satisfaction: A comprehensive analysis of PTCL after its privatization. *International Letters of Social and Humanistic Sciences, 51*, 95–105.

Malik, M. S., Basit, A. B., & Qazi, A. K. (2011). Unions and management: A case study of Pakistan Telecommunication Corporation. *Pakistan Journal of Social Sciences, 31*(1), 185–199.

Siddiqi, M. F., Nouman, M., & Ahmad, A. (2012). Does privatization affect performance? *Journal of Managerial Sciences, 6*(2), 190.

Siddiqui, K., & Mangi, R. A. (2013). Failure of corporate governance: Privatization of PTCL Pakistan. *The IUP Journal of Corporate Governance, 13*, 62–69.

CHAPTER 9

Financial Sector Case Studies

Abstract The transition of Pakistan's financial industry from state-controlled to privately owned entities through privatization has yielded diverse outcomes. Through a historical lens, this chapter analyses the impact of privatization on the financial sector in Pakistan, focusing on case studies of Allied Bank Limited (ABL) and Habib Bank Limited (HBL). The chapter outlines the challenges faced by ABL post-privatization, including a surge in non-performing loans (NPLs) and financial losses. This led to significant restructuring efforts by the State Bank of Pakistan (SBP) to stabilize the bank's operations and prepare it for re-privatization. In contrast, HBL's privatization experience, marked by management control transfer to Aga Khan Fund for Economic Development (AKFED), resulted in a swift turnaround and notable improvements in financial performance." In light of these insights, the chapter advocates for a refined approach to privatization, one that carefully balances privatization objectives with broader economic development goals and ensures the resilience of the financial system.

Keywords Financial Industry • Financial Sector in Pakistan • Allied Bank Limited (ABL) • Habib Bank Limited (HBL) • State Bank of Pakistan (SBP) Restructuring Efforts • Financial System Resilience

G. Samad, N. Faraz, *The Face of Privatization in Pakistan*,
https://doi.org/10.1007/978-981-97-8385-4_9

Privatization History

The early 1970s saw significant changes in the financial sector of Pakistan due to the nationalization of domestic banks under the Banks Nationalization Act of 1974. The Pakistan Banking Council (PBC) was formed to serve as a holding company for nationalized commercial banks and to act as a supervisory body. Six main national commercial banks were formed out of all the nationalized domestic banks, while numerous specialized credit institutions were also established.

The main goals of nationalization of the banking sector included the provision of a source of funding to the government, and to direct bank credit toward particular emerging industries. Thus, at the start of 1990s, the financial industry was dominated by the public sector banks with a share of 92.2% in the total assets of the whole banking sector (Table 9.1).

However, it was realized by the end of the 1980s that the socio-economic goals sought out through the nationalization of the banking sector were not being met. The dominance of the public sector in the financial sector, along with direct monetary control tools, were "supposed" to cause financial suppression, inefficiency, displacement of the private sector, and a significant drop in asset quality.

Resultantly, financial deregulation was carried out under the IMF's SAP in early 1990s, resulting in the privatization of all major commercial banks except National Bank of Pakistan (NBP). According to Dr. Ishrat Hussain (former governor SBP), "the Government of Pakistan has decided to privatize the public sector banks because of lack of financial discipline owing to undue political interference in the financial intermediation process. The public sector banks were the major sources of bad loans, accounting for 90% of bad loans in the entire system, and were the main loss-makers."

The privatization of banks started in 1991, first with the privatization of ABL, by selling 51% of its shares to the EMG group, then moving

Table 9.1 Financial status of banking system before privatization

Banks	*Assets (million rupees)*	*Deposits (million rupees)*	*Equity (million rupees)*
Public	392.3	329.7	14.9
International	33.4	24.7	2.5
Private	0	0	0

Source: Husain, (2004)

Table 9.2 Privatization of Commercial Banks

Banks	*Sale Price (million PKR)*	*Date of transfer*	*Buyer name*
Allied Bank Limited (51%)	972	Feb 1991	EMG
Muslim Commercial Bank (75%)	2420	April 1991	National Group
Bankers Equity Ltd. (51%)	619	June 1996	LTV Group
Habib Credit & Exchange 70 % (52,500,000)	1634	July 1997	Sh. Nahyan bin Mubarik Al-Nahyan
United Bank Ltd. 51% (264,180,000 shares)	12,350	October 2002	Consortium of Bestway & Abu Dhabi Group
Bank Alfalah 30% (22,500,000 shares)	620	December 2002	Abu Dhabi Group
Habib Bank Ltd. 51% (351,900,000 shares)	22,409	December 2003	Agha Khan Fund for Economic Development
Total	41,023		

Source: Privatization Commission of Pakistan

toward MCB, selling 75% of its shares to the National Group. In 2002, the UBL was sold off to the consortium of Bestway and Abu Dhabi Group, while HBL was sold off to Agha Khan Fund for Economic Development (AKFED) in 2003. The details have been given in Table 9.2.

Having said this, it is important to analyze the performance of the banking sector after financial sector reforms. We have focused on the case studies of ABL and HBL, because as per popular opinion, HBL improved its balance sheet and turned into financially sound firms after privatization. However, ABL lagged behind, exhibiting no meaningful improvement in its operations and continuing to lose money virtually at the same rate as when it was in the public ownership.

Privatization Experience of ABL

ABL started its operations in 1942 in Lahore by the name of Australasia Bank, and was performing better until 1974. Under the nationalization policy, it was merged with other three small banks, ranking it amongst one of the five big National Commercial Banks (NCBs) of the country. The era of nationalization was considered to be the nightmare for the government and frequent bank bailouts became a norm.

Resultantly, during 1990s when privatization was on its peak, ABL was also put on the list of potential candidates for privatization. Thus, 26% of the shares of ABL were transferred to the employees' management group of ABL in 1991. In 1993, another 25% shares were again transferred to the same group. At the time of the transfer, non-performing loans made up 16% of the loan book, which, a decade later in 2003, reached a record high at 44%. In 1999, it was discovered that one of ABL's biggest defaulters had acquired around 35–40% of the company's stock from its employees. Therefore, State Bank had to establish limitations on the transfer of shares from employees to non-employees in July 1999, barring any transfers without prior SBP clearance. The bank's first two post-privatization CEOs had also been imprisoned for corruption charges at the end of their terms in office.

In light of these circumstances, the State Bank suggested to the Privatization Commission to transfer the sale of ABL to SBP and remove the name of ABL from the list of privatizations. As a result, ABL was removed from the list, and the remaining 49% shares were transferred to SBP in 2003. SBP started the process of rebuilding the bank and transferring ownership to an established private sector financial institution that would buy significant stakes in the company. As a result, it prequalified six parties in February 2004 to compete for the 49% of ABL's shares. Finally, its ownership was transferred to Ibrahim Group.

Table 9.3 shows the performance of ABL in the years, right after privatization. In terms of non-performing loans (NPLs), the situation got severely deteriorated. Only slight improvement could be observed in the percentage share of assets and deposits of ABL in those of NCBs. Advances, which had grown a little at first, fell off in later years.

The profitability of ABL also decreased as a result of the rising NPLs; the bank had significant losses between 2000 and 2002. Only after the

Table 9.3 Post-Privatization Financial Performance of ABL

Performance Indicators	*1994*	*1997*	*2000*	*2003*
Assets (%age of assets of NCBs)	9.6	10.4	11.7	12.2
Deposits (%age of deposits of NCBs)	9.8	10.6	13	14.3
Advances (%age of Advances of NCBs)	10.9	12.5	14.2	11.2
NPLs (%age of total loans)	16.6	17.9	29.4	43.8

Source: Husain, (2004)

SBP replaced the old Board of Directors with a new one in 2001, did things start to get better. Since 1999, the ROA has been negative, and it wasn't until 2003 that the bank started to turn into a profit. Net profit showed an increasing trend afterward. NPL ratio also started to decrease afterward as shown in Figs. 9.1 and 9.2. It was 2.04% in 2021.

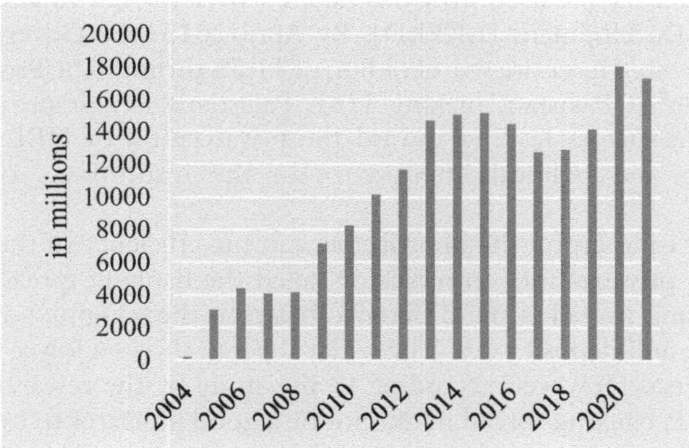

Fig. 9.1 Net Profit/loss

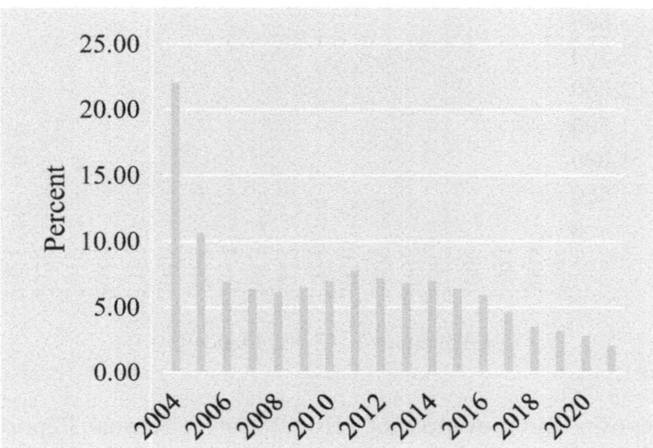

Fig. 9.2 NPL ratio

Privatization Experience of HBL

HBL was founded before partition in 1941, but shifted its operations to Pakistan after independence. It was the first commercial bank to lay its foundation in the country. It opened its first international branch in Colombo, Sri Lanka, in 1951. It was nationalized in 1974 under the nationalization program. However, in February 2004, the bank was privatized and management control was handed over to Aga Khan Fund for Economic Development (AKFED). By April 2015, the Government of Pakistan divested its entire shareholding of 41.5% through the Privatization Commission of Pakistan, making HBL Pakistan's largest private bank. Some of the factors leading toward the privatization of HBL included overstaffing and political interference in the institution's operations (Fig. 9.3).

In order to interpret the improvement in the efficiency of the banking sector after privatization, an indicator called the banking spread is being used. Banking spread is the difference between the weighted average of the lending and deposit rates. The wider the gap shows a lower efficiency and vice versa. However, according to the study by the research department of SBP, banking spread might not be a good indicator to capture the

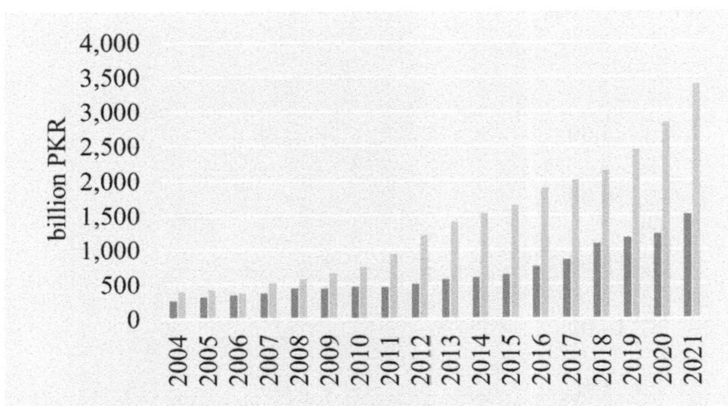

Fig. 9.3 Deposits and Advances of HBL. (Source: Annual Reports of HBL, 2004–2021)

efficiency of the banking sector since it does not represent all the earnings and expenses of a bank. The report further mentions that a broader term, that is, ***interest rate spread*** might serve as a better alternative. Thus, we have constructed interest rate spread to gauge the efficiency of HBL after privatization.

According to the annual financial statements of HBL from 2004 to 2021, deposits and advances have increased over time. However, increase in the deposits has been more than the increase in the advances. On the opposite side, we can see that interest earnings from borrowings have been more than the interest payments to the depositors, which roughly shows that the interest rate spread has been high over the period after the privatization. In order to get a clear picture, have a look at interest spread in Figs. 9.4 and 9.5 which also shows that from 2004 to 2011, the interest rate spread has been wider. However, it got narrower till 2019 but increased once again in 2020 and 2021.

From the analysis of both the banks, we have noticed that HBL, unlike ABL, improved its performance quickly after privatization. ABL took years to get on track and embark upon the path of financial development.

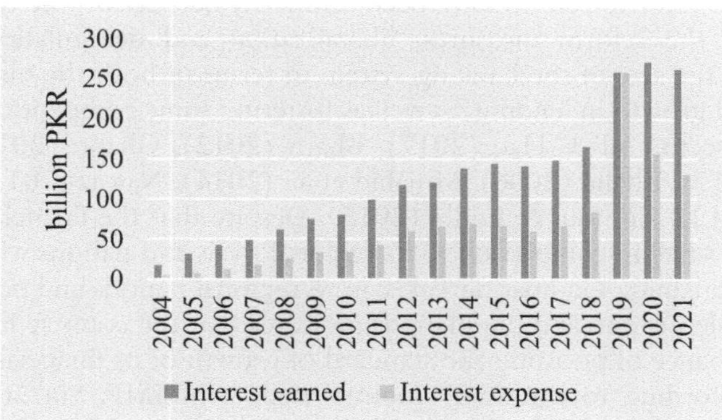

Fig. 9.4 Interest earned/expense of HBL. (*Source*: Annual Reports of HBL, 2004–2021)

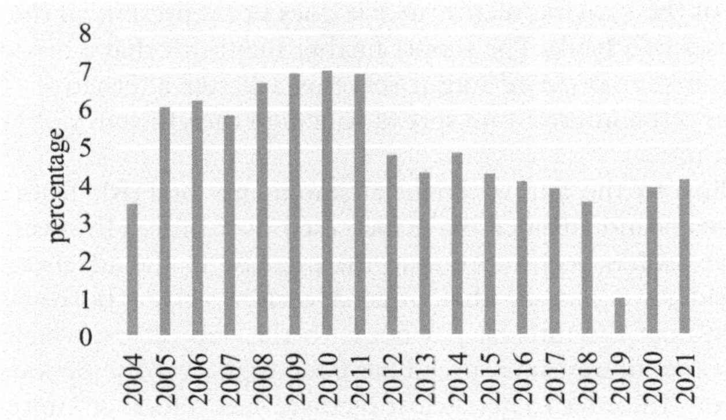

Fig. 9.5 Interest rate Spread of HBL. (*Source*: Annual Reports of HBL, 2004–2021)

Concluding Remarks

The financial sector in Pakistan has significantly expanded due to extensive financial reforms. The weaknesses and inefficiencies that plagued banking operations prior to reform have been drastically decreased. The two main pillars of the reform measures, liberalization and deregulation, have increased the size of the banking system in terms of both the number of banks and growth in lending, as well as fostering some competition in the banking sector Ali & Haq (2017), Bhatti (2012), Ghauri (2013), Ijaz et al. (2012), Khalid (2006), Mujahid et al. (2014), Nawaz (2011), Shah et al. (2012), Siddiqui & Lodhi (2015). Despite that the financial sector remained small in comparison to its regional rivals and nations with comparable dynamics. Comparing Pakistan to regional nations and peers with comparable income and populations indicates that the country has a significant chance of boosting the standard of growth of its financial institutions. According to the Staff Country Report of IMF, "in 2014, the indices of financial institutions in Asia and Pacific and in the Emerging Market economies exceeded that of Pakistan by 54 percent and 71 percent, respectively. The rankings of South Asian peers such as Bangladesh, India, and Sri Lanka were 7 to 33 percent higher. After the global financial crisis, financial institutions in all peer economies have sizably improved, while Pakistan's index initially fell and by 2014 had just recovered to pre-crisis levels."

Therefore, reforming the financial industry in Pakistan is still a work in progress. The sector must continue to be responsive and supportive of the larger economic agenda given the shifting dynamics of the economy, its increasing complexity, and related risks.

References

Ali, H., & Haq, A. U. (2017). Impact of privatization of banks on profitability. *Scientific Journal of Management and Social Sciences, 1*(1), 24–35.

Bhatti, N. (2012). measuring performance, efficiency of allied & Muslim commercial banks before after privatization period. *Journal of Asian Business Strategy, 2*(1), 24–37.

Ghauri, S. M. (2013). Does privatization really work? Study of Pakistan's banking sector. *The Interenational Journal of Management, 2*(1), 1–14.

Husain, I. (2004, April). Policy considerations before bank privatization country experience. In *World Bank, IMF and Brookings Instituion conference on Role of State-owned Financial Instituions Policy and Practice, April* (pp. 26–27).

Ijaz, D., Naseem, M. A., & Iqbal, J. (2012). Impact of privatization on non-performing loans of conventional commercial banks in Pakistan. *Academic Research International, 3*(1), 322.

Khalid, U. (2006). The effect of privatization and liberalization on banking sector performance in Pakistan. *SBP Research Bulletin, 2*(2), 403–425.

Mujahid, M., Hashmi, F. K. H., & Abbas, M. D. (2014). Impact of privatization of banks on profitability of banking sector in Pakistan. *Journal of Economics and Sustainable Development, 5*(24), 101–110.

Nawaz, A. (2011). *Pakistani's banking sector privatization experience* (Doctoral dissertation, KDI School).

Shah, A. A., Naqvi, S. A. H., & Shaikh, F. M. (2012). Comparative analysis of performance efficiency of allied & Muslim commercial banks before and after the privatization period. *Journal of Business Strategies, 6*(1), 16.

Siddiqui, S., & Lodhi, S. (2015). Impact of privatization on firm's performance: A case of banking sector of Pakistan. *International of Journal of Multidisciplinary and Current Research, 3*(2), 2–16.

PART IV

Legal Framework of Privatization

CHAPTER 10

State-Owned Enterprises (Governance and Operations) Act, 2023

Abstract The role of effective governance, transparency, and accountability in the operations of SOEs is of paramount importance. However, the operational efficiency, transparency, and governance of SOEs have been marred by challenges, necessitating a critical analysis of the SOEs Act of 2023 to enhance governance standards and ensure optimal performance. This chapter provides an in-depth review of the SOEs Act of 2023 in Pakistan, focusing on its key features, provisions, and implications for governing SOEs. It digs into various aspects of the Act, including SOE management policies, criteria for prudent management practices, performance measurement requirements, board member appointments, financial transparency, shareholding rights, and performance monitoring. This chapter adding the flavor on how government is aiming to enhance governance standards and ensure optimal performance of public sector enterprises in Pakistan.

Keywords SOEs Governance • Transparency • Operational Efficiency • SOEs Act • Public Sector Enterprises in Pakistan

The governance and management of SOEs are critical to ensure their efficiency, transparency, and accountability, as well as to prevent corruption and misuse of public funds. The legal framework governing state-owned enterprises (SOEs) in Pakistan is primarily composed of the

G. Samad, N. Faraz, *The Face of Privatization in Pakistan*,
https://doi.org/10.1007/978-981-97-8385-4_10

Companies Act, 2017, the Public Sector Companies (Corporate Governance) Rules 2013, and the state-owned companies (Corporate Governance) Rules 2018. These laws are intended to provide a legal framework for the governance, operations, and control of SOEs, including their boards and management. Additionally, the government has issued various policy directives and guidelines to improve the performance and accountability of SOEs in the country. The recent SOEs Act, 2023, is an important piece of legislation that sets out the legal framework for the establishment, management, and oversight of SOEs. In this review, we will examine the key provisions of the SOEs Act and assess its effectiveness in achieving the objectives of good governance, transparency, and accountability (Finance Division, 2023).

Features of SOEs Act, 2023

The Act, which governs the operations of SOEs in Pakistan, is structured into 11 comprehensive chapters. These chapters are subdivided into sections and sub-sections to provide a detailed account of various aspects pertaining to SOE activities. The provisions outlined within each section and sub-section offer an in-depth understanding of the legal framework that guides these enterprises' functioning across different domains. While the SOEs Act, 2023, provides a comprehensive framework for the ownership, governance, and management of state-owned enterprises, there are certain gaps and confusions that need to be addressed.

General Provisions

According to the general provisions which is provided in Chap. 1 of the SOEs Act, this Act will apply to all public sector companies (mentioned in the Companies Act, 2017) regardless of any other conflicting provisions in other laws that may be currently in force. In other words, if there are any existing laws or regulations that seem to contradict the provisions of the State-Owned Enterprises Act, those conflicting laws will not take precedence over this act. Instead, this act will supersede any such conflicting provisions and govern the functioning of all public sector companies. However, this Act will not be applicable to the regulatory bodies that have specific powers to issue licenses, grant tariffs, or conduct investigations related to non-compliance with their statutory functions and powers. Furthermore, this act will not be applicable to enterprises providing health and educational services, and to any other SOE which is specifically excluded from the complete or partial application of this Act.

Based on the provisions related to the scope of SOEs in the SOE Act, there are a few potential loopholes or areas that may warrant further consideration.

The Act states that it will supersede any conflicting provisions in other laws, but it is not clear how such conflicts will be resolved. This could potentially lead to legal challenges or confusion in the interpretation and application of the Act.

The Act exempts regulatory bodies from its application, which may limit the ability of the Act to promote good governance and sound management practices in sectors that are heavily regulated.

SOE Management Policy and Principles

According to the Act, the federal government is required to design an SOE ownership and management policy, at least once in every five years, which mainly aims at:

- Clarifying shareholding responsibilities of the federal government
- Ensuring effective management of the fiscal risks associated with the SOEs
- Ensuring that the federal government acts as an informed and active shareholder

Apart from the above, there is a list of some other aspects mentioned in the Act, to be covered in the policy. However, there are some aspects which have been overlooked to be included in the policy namely,

The Act is silent on encouraging or incentivizing the SOEs to invest in research and development, innovation, or the adoption of new technologies, which could limit their ability to adapt to changing market conditions and to remain competitive.

Additionally, the Act does not mention that the policy should include rules regarding the demonstration of social and environmental responsibility by the SOEs, such as reducing their carbon footprint, promoting gender equality, or supporting community development, which could limit their ability to contribute to sustainable and inclusive economic growth.

Prudent and Efficient Management

In order to promote accountability, transparency, and efficiency in the management of public assets, the Act includes provisions related to sound and prudent management (section 6, sub-section 2(c)).

However, the Act has not provided detailed provisions on how SOEs should manage their workforce, including issues such as recruitment, training, and performance management.

According to the Act, the primary objective of an SOE is to operate in an efficient manner, taking into account the economic consequences of any decision in the long run. It also mentions that an SOE should take into account the communal and environmental effects of its operations. Furthermore, it should maintain high standards of business conduct. According to the sub-section 7(4) of the Act, the federal government shall not require a commercial SOE to undertake a public service obligation which deviates from its primary objective.

While the objectives of SOEs as defined by the Act are generally sound, there are some potential loopholes or limitations that should be considered.

The objectives of the SOEs must include balancing commercial performance with public policy goals, despite the fact that there may be a tension between these two objectives. But if commercial performance is prioritized over public policy goals, there is a risk that SOEs may operate in a way that is not in the best interests of the public.

Measurable Performance

The provisions require an SOE and its subsidiaries to have a solid business plan for three years at the start of every financial year. The business plan has to be designed in consultation of the respective division and the draft has to be shared with the CMU for further analysis. The plan should contain information about the operations, and strategic direction of that SOE. Additionally, it should contain information on the financial and non-financial performance of the SOE as well.

However, the Act does not provide any guidance on how the business plan should be structured or what specific information it should include, beyond general references to operations, strategic direction, and performance. Furthermore, the paragraph does not specify the timeframe or deadlines for submitting the business plan, or the consequences of failing to comply with this requirement.

Responsible Management

Chapter 5 includes clauses related to the appointment of chairman, directors, and independent directors of the board of every SOE, criteria for their qualification and disqualification, and the terms of office of the directors.

Financial Transparency

The chapter on financial transparency requires SOEs to maintain accurate and transparent financial records, including the disclosure of financial statements, budgets, and audit reports. However, there are some potential areas where the chapter on financial transparency in the Act could be improved or expanded.

In section 25(2), it has been mentioned that SOEs must maintain accurate and transparent financial records, including the disclosure of financial statements, budgets, and audit reports. However, it should also specify the responsibilities of auditors and it should require them to be independent and objective in their assessments of SOEs' financial statements.

Another area for improvement could be the level of detail required in financial reporting. The Act could require SOEs to disclose not only their financial statements but also information on their procurement processes, contracts, and other financial transactions to ensure greater transparency and accountability.

Lastly, the Act could also specify the consequences for non-compliance with financial reporting requirements, such as fines or other penalties, to ensure that SOEs are incentivized to comply with the financial transparency provisions.

Shareholding Rights of the Federal Government

This part of SOEs Act provides provisions related to the role of the federal government as a shareholder in the SOEs. Based on best practices in corporate governance, there are several other potential provisions that could be included in the chapter on the shareholding rights of the federal government in SOEs, Act in Pakistan.

The Act requires that the federal government has the right to direct an SOE to disclose specified information related to the affairs of that SOE. However, it should also specify the methods and frequency of communication between the federal government and the SOE to ensure that the government is kept informed of the SOE's performance and strategic direction.

Sub-section 30 (c) requires that the government must not direct the disclosure of information relating to an individual if the individual is identifiable from the information. However, in case of corruption, the Act should require that the SOE implement anti-corruption measures, including the disclosure of related-party transactions and the establishment of a code of ethics for employees and directors.

Additionally, the Act could specify the procedures for resolving disputes between the federal government and other shareholders of the SOE, including the appointment of an independent arbitrator or mediator.

Monitoring Performance

Chapter 9 of the SOEs Act, 2023, contains provisions related to monitoring the performance of the SOEs. For this, the federal government is required to establish a central monitoring unit (CMU) in the finance division. A CMU should have all the data related to the financial and operational performance of the SOEs. On the basis of this data, the CMU is required to analyze the performance of the SOEs against their set targets, and report that to the federal government.

The SOEs are also required to provide the CMU with all the information. If there is any change in the already provided data, the SOE must update it within 15 days of such a change.

However, to be more specific, the Act should define the key performance indicators (KPIs) and metrics that will be used to evaluate the performance of SOEs, such as financial performance, operational efficiency, social and environmental impact, and customer satisfaction. Furthermore, the Act should specify the criteria and benchmarks against which the SOEs will be evaluated, based on their size, sector, and strategic goals. Based on the evaluation, the Act should outline the consequences of poor performance, such as penalties, sanctions, or restructuring measures, to ensure that SOEs are held accountable for their actions and decisions. On the contrary, the Act should also encourage the use of performance-based incentives, such as bonuses or stock options, to reward SOE managers and employees for achieving or exceeding their performance targets.

References

Finance Division (2023). https://www.finance.gov.pk/SOEs_Act_2023.pdf

CHAPTER 11

Role of Privatization Commission

Abstract A robust legal framework is paramount for the successful implementation of privatization initiatives. Chapter 11 provides an extensive overview of the intricate legal landscape surrounding privatization in Pakistan, tracing the evolution of laws and regulations governing this transformative process. It meticulously examines key enactments such as the Transfer of Managed Establishments Order of 1978, which initially vested significant powers in the federal government regarding privatization. The discussion extends to the Privatization Commission Ordinance of 2000, pivotal for consolidating commissions and empowering the Privatization Commission with enhanced authority.

Moreover, the chapter sheds light on recent amendments to the Privatization Commission Ordinance in 2021, aiming to bolster the commission's autonomy, simplify procedures, and safeguard employee rights amidst privatization efforts. It introduces the Inter-governmental Commercial Transactions Act of 2022, delineating pathways for state asset privatization through government-to-government agreements.

Keywords Privatization Framework • Privatization Commission Ordinance • Privatization Commission Ordinance in 2021 • Autonomy • Privatization Procedures • Inter-governmental Commercial Transactions Act of 2022

G. Samad, N. Faraz, *The Face of Privatization in Pakistan*,
https://doi.org/10.1007/978-981-97-8385-4_11

The legal framework for privatization in Pakistan has undergone several changes over the years, with the government enacting laws and regulations to facilitate the privatization process. This chapter provides an overview of the legal framework of privatization in Pakistan, including the laws and regulations governing the process, the role of regulatory bodies, and the legal protections available to investors.

While the legal framework of privatization in Pakistan is intended to ensure a fair and transparent process, there have been some challenges and loopholes in its implementation. For instance, some critics have argued that the privatization process has not always been conducted in a transparent manner, leading to concerns over corruption and the misuse of public resources. Additionally, there have been cases where privatized entities have failed to perform as expected, leading to questions over the effectiveness of the privatization process. This chapter also discusses some of the challenges and criticisms of the legal framework of privatization in Pakistan, including issues around transparency, accountability, and the regulation of privatized entities.

Transfer of Managed Establishment's Order, 1978

As already mentioned that the wave of privatization in Pakistan could be observed properly in the late 1970s with the promulgation of the President's Order called the *Transfer of Managed Establishments Order, 1978*. The Order was amended in 1991 under the title *Transfer of Managed Establishments (Amendment) Act, 1991*. Some of the main features of the Order are as follows:

Powers of Federal Government

According to the Order, the federal government had absolute powers of offering the rights and shares of the nationalized industries to their previous owners. In case of non-interest of the previous owners, the federal government was free to transfer the shares and propriety rights to any other party on the terms and conditions it deemed fit. In case the employees of the company offered the higher bid, the government was free not to make the offer to its previous owners.

Rights of the Stakeholders

On the rights of the stakeholders, especially labor and employees of the managed establishment, the Order guaranteed them to continue their service on the previous rules and conditions. For this, an Inter-ministerial Committee was formed to deal with the issues of the labor employed. The employees/labor were ensured:

- A minimum one-year service guarantee to the employees after privatization.
- Reservation of the right of 10% shares of the employees/labor.
- The right to the employees to offer the bid for the purchase of a certain unit.
- Golden Handshake Scheme (GHS) and Voluntary Separation Scheme (VSS).

Box 11.1 Powers of the Privatization Commission

- Developing and implementing policies for the privatization of state-owned assets and enterprises.
- Conducting feasibility studies and valuations of state-owned assets and enterprises.
- Approving and recommending privatization plans and transactions to the federal government for approval.
- Managing and executing the privatization process, including the selection of financial advisers, legal advisers, and other professionals required for the transaction.
- Approving the terms of privatization transactions, including the sale price, payment terms, and other contractual terms.
- Facilitating the transfer of ownership and control of privatized assets and enterprises to private sector buyers.
- Monitoring and reporting on the progress of privatization transactions and the performance of privatized enterprises.
- Recommending and implementing measures

Privatization Commission Ordinance, 2000

Initially there were two commissions: one dealing with the privatization of banks, financial institutions, and industrial sector, and another dealing with the power sector. On top of these, there were individual committees dealing with privatization of telecom and transportation sector. However, all these individual commissions were brought under a single umbrella of the *Privatization Commission (PC)* at the end of 1993. There was a Cabinet Committee on Privatization (CCoP) dealing with the approval of the recommendations of the PC. However, in order to make it an autonomous/semi-autonomous body, the *Privatization Commission Ordinance, 2000* was promulgated, leading toward strengthening of the legal powers of PC.

In order to provide more autonomy and flexibility to the *PC* in carrying out the privatization process in the country, the Ordinance was amended in 2021 under *Privatization Commission Ordinance (Amendment Act), 2021*. Some of the key features of the amendment act are:

Main Features of Privatization Commission Ordinance (Amendment Act), 2021

1. ***Enhanced Powers:*** The amendment act has expanded the jurisdiction of the Privatization Commission by granting it more autonomy and enhanced powers to carry out the privatization process.
2. ***Utilization of Privatization Proceeds***: The Ordinance mentions that the privatization proceeds of privatization will be used for paying of the federal government debt (90%), and alleviating poverty (10%).
3. ***Privatization Fund:*** Under section 16 of the Ordinance, the Commission has to establish a Privatization Fund for depositing the privatization proceeds and has the powers to withdraw/contribute any amount from the fund whenever necessary.
4. ***Modes of Privatization:*** Section 25 mentions the modes of privatization, where the PC is empowered to adopt any one of them. These include sale of assets and business, sale of shares through auction/tender, public offer of shares through stock exchange, sale to the employees/management of the SOE, lease, and any other method prescribed.

5. ***Simplification of Procedures:*** The amendment act has simplified the procedures of the privatization process by allowing the Commission to directly initiate the process without seeking prior approval from the Cabinet.
6. ***Protection of Employee Rights:*** The amendment act has put in place safeguards to protect the rights of employees who may be affected by the privatization process.
7. ***Exemption from Taxes:*** According to section 44, PC is exempted of any kind of taxes, levies, charges on any of its business assets, income, or wealth.

Overall, the Privatization Commission Ordinance (Amendment Act), 2021, aims to increase the efficiency of the privatization process in the country and attract more foreign and domestic investors to invest in the privatization of state-owned enterprises. However, in case of any doubts in the transaction, the federal government or any of its agencies has the right to investigate the matter within a year. After one year, the rights to investigate will be expired.

Inter-governmental Commercial Transactions Act, 2022

Last year, another ordinance has been approved by the Cabinet, according to which the federal government is empowered to privatize state assets under the framework of G2G agreement. The main features of the Act are follows:

- The federal government has discretionary powers to sell state assets to the governments of the friendly countries.
- The federal government has the power to relax or exempt any regulatory requirement mentioned in any other state law in order to implement the inter-governmental transaction.
- The ordinance prohibits legal action against those who are involved in inter-governmental transaction, and indemnification has been expanded to cover up the mistakes in procedure or failures to perform. Similar to this, unless there is "evidence" of personal financial gain, neither an investigating agency nor any court can begin an investigation into any procedural irregularity.

- Furthermore, the Act will remain effective regardless of any contradiction it may have with the Privatization Commission Ordinance, 2000, Companies Act, 2017, SECP Act, 1997, Securities Act, 2015, or any other existing laws.

Loopholes in the Laws of Privatization

While the Privatization Commission Ordinance (Amendment Act), 2021, aims to improve the privatization process in Pakistan, there may be some loopholes or potential limitations that could impact its effectiveness. Here are some possible loopholes:

- **The acts/ordinances mentioned above are not clear on what the federal government can or cannot sell. Similarly, no solid basis/ reason for privatizing a particular entity is mentioned in the law.**

If the reason is that we have run out of the domestic/foreign reserves, and the ultimate solution is to divest the state assets, then the policy is poorly comprehended. Similarly, servicing the debt through the sale of state assets on easy terms is of high concern for the nation. Poverty alleviation objective is added up just to cover-up the loopholes in the privatization policy.

Furthermore, it is true that running an enterprise is not the basic role of the government to play until it is some exceptional case, but regulating a business and policymaking are the core government duties to fulfill. Therefore, privatization must be linked with the role of government which it has to play, and not with the sale of nation's assets to service the debt.

- **The immunity against any legal proceedings given to the parties involved in the sale of state assets is not commendable.**

The clause barring any legal proceedings is a dangerous precedent which has been set, and thus is raising a high transparency concern as it can lead to inefficient and incompetent deals. Incompetent parties can take undue advantage of this clause. Therefore, there must be some element of accountability involved, specifically in case of the deals with the foreign nations, which also involve a high security concern Naveed et al. (2018), Waseem & Hussain (2019).

- **Exempting the PC from any kind of taxes is not acceptable.**

On one hand, the absolute powers given to PC to use the resources of the PC Fund whenever it feels the need of can lead to fraud and corruption. While on the other, the absolute exemption from all kinds of taxes is creating confusion. Exemption must be given under exceptional circumstances, for instance, if the entity is of highly productive nature and needs support from the government, or is working in an area where free market rules cannot be applied. Otherwise, unconditional exemptions do not make much sense.

- The amendment act does not provide clear guidelines to ensure transparency in the privatization process which can be misused by those involved in the process.
- With the increased autonomy given to the Privatization Commission, there is a possibility for corruption as there may not be sufficient checks and balances in place.
- While the amendment act includes provisions to protect employee rights, it may not be enough as the privatization process can often result in job losses or reduced benefits for employees.
- The amendment act does not provide clear guidelines on how to value state-owned assets, which could result in the undervaluation of assets and loss of revenue for the government.
- The amendment act may not have provisions in place to ensure local participation in the privatization process, which can result in foreign entities acquiring local assets without adequate consideration of domestic interests.
- The amendment act does not provide a clear regulatory oversight mechanism to ensure that the privatization process is conducted in a fair and transparent manner, which could lead to abuse of power or unfair practices.
- The privatization of certain state-owned entities could lead to a reduction in public services such as water, electricity, or healthcare, which could negatively impact the public.
- **Marginalization of Certain Groups:** There is a possibility that certain marginalized groups, such as workers, minorities, or women, could be disproportionately affected by the privatization process.

- **Impact on National Security:** The privatization of certain industries or entities, such as the defense or strategic industries, could potentially have an impact on national security if it is not conducted with proper oversight and consideration.

It is important to note that while these potential loopholes exist, they do not necessarily negate the benefits of the Privatization Commission Ordinance (Amendment Act), 2021. Privatization is an economic policy tool of central importance, where decisions regarding individual SOEs must be made on case-to-case basis. The policy can help a lot of people, but its success depends on having clear goals, a good strategy, and a transparent process. For this, the legal framework for privatization should have clarity with respect to all the matters related to public concern. It should also need to have a clause on regulating the post-privatization procedures of the SOEs. Most importantly, it should clearly specify what kind of business can/cannot be privatized taking into account the security and strategic concerns. Furthermore, it is important for the government to closely monitor the implementation of the Privatization Commission Ordinance (Amendment Act), 2021, to ensure that it achieves its intended objectives and does not have any negative consequences.

References

Naveed, S., Salman, Y., Jabeen, N., Jadoon, M. Z. I., & Irfan, S. (2018). Governance and management of state-owned enterprises in Pakistan. *Pakistan Economic and Social Review, 56*(1), 47–66.

Waseem, M. A., & Hussain, S. (2019). Importance of judicial activism to ensure transparency in Pakistan: A case study on privatization of Pakistan Steel Mills Case 2006. *Journal of History Culture and Art Research, 8*(2), 62–84.

CHAPTER 12

Public-private Partnerships

Abstract Limited success of privatization efforts in Pakistan has prompted a growing emphasis on Public-Private Partnerships (PPPs) as a viable alternative. In Pakistan, PPPs have gained traction since the 1990s, particularly in sectors like transportation, energy, healthcare, education, and water management. The chapter presents the state of PPPs, both globally and within Pakistan, offering a comprehensive analysis of their evolution, types, legal frameworks, successes, challenges, and strategies for effective implementation. Globally, PPPs have emerged as essential tools for infrastructure development, showcasing their effectiveness in various sectors like transportation, healthcare, education, water management, and energy, with tangible benefits such as cost savings and improved service quality. The establishment of the Public-Private Partnership Authority (P3A) underscores the government's commitment to fostering partnerships and streamlining PPP processes. The legal framework for PPPs in Pakistan comprises various laws, policies, and guidelines at federal and provincial levels, providing clarity and guidance for PPP projects. The chapter further outlines successful PPP projects in Pakistan while also addressing persistent challenges like political instability, procurement complexities, risk allocation, financing constraints, capacity limitations, and social/environmental concerns.

G. Samad, N. Faraz, *The Face of Privatization in Pakistan*, https://doi.org/10.1007/978-981-97-8385-4_12

Keywords Public-Private Partnerships (PPPs) • PPPs in Pakistan • Types of PPPs • Legal Frameworks for PPPs • Public-Private Partnership Authority (P3A) • Federal and Provincial PPP • PPP Projects in Pakistan

Public-Private Partnerships (PPPs) have emerged as a critical tool in addressing the growing demand for infrastructure-related services, particularly in sectors where intensive capital investment is necessary. The involvement of the private sector enables governments to leverage their resources and expertise, facilitating efficient project delivery while maintaining high-quality standards. Moreover, PPPs offer an effective collaboration framework between public and private entities that can significantly improve service delivery outcomes across various industries. This approach has been successful worldwide, with numerous examples demonstrating its potential benefits in both developed and developing nations Anas et al. (2017), Arpita (2022), Bilal et al. (2018).

This chapter explores the scope of PPPs globally and examines their impact on enhancing service quality. Most importantly, it assesses the extent to which this model's success supports its usefulness for Pakistan's unique needs regarding sustainable development initiatives.

International Evidence on PPPs

PPPs in the Developed World

PPPs have been prevalent in the developed countries, particularly Europe and North America. According to the World Bank, Europe is the largest market for PPPs, accounting for over half of all PPP projects globally. The UK, Spain, and France are the largest PPP markets in Europe. Here are a few examples of the PPP projects in different sectors in the developed world.

- ***Transportation Sector:*** Transportation sector is the most common sector for PPPs in the developed world, particularly for large-scale projects such as toll roads, bridges, and tunnels. This is likely because transportation infrastructure requires large amounts of capital investment and is often too expensive for governments to finance on their own. Transportation accounts for around 60% of all PPP projects in

Box 12.1 Examples of PPPs in the Transportation Sector in the Developed World

Here are some successful examples of PPPs in the transportation sector in the developed world:

1. Heathrow Airport Terminal 5, UK: This PPP involved the construction of a new terminal at Heathrow Airport in London. The project was led by the airport operator, BAA, and involved several private companies, including construction firm Laing O'Rourke and engineering firm Arup.
2. Eurotunnel, France/UK: The Eurotunnel is a cross-Channel rail link between the UK and France. It was built and is operated by a private company, Eurotunnel Group, under a PPP agreement with the governments of the UK and France.
3. High Speed 1, UK: This PPP involved the construction of a high-speed rail link between London and the Channel Tunnel. The project was led by the government-owned company HS1 Ltd., with private sector partners including engineering firms Bechtel and Halcrow.
4. Sydney Metro, Australia: The Sydney Metro is a new rapid transit system being built in Sydney, Australia. The project is being delivered under a PPP agreement between the government of New South Wales and private sector consortium Northwest Rapid Transit.
5. Denver FasTracks, USA: The Denver FasTracks project is a regional rail and bus system being built in the Denver metropolitan area. The project is being delivered under a PPP agreement between the Regional Transportation District and private sector partners, including engineering firm Fluor Corporation.

OECD countries. A study by the European Investment Bank found that PPPs for transportation infrastructure in Europe have led to cost savings of up to 20% compared to traditional public procurement. Furthermore, PPPs generate significant economic benefits, including job creation and increased economic activity. It is found that PPPs for transportation infrastructure in Europe have led to the creation of over 100,000 jobs.

Box 12.2 PPPs in the Health Sector in the Developed World

PPPs in the health sector in the developed world have been used to develop modern healthcare facilities and provide high-quality care to patients. However, PPPs in the health sector can be complex and require careful consideration of the specific context and the risks and benefits involved. Here are some examples of PPPs in the health sector in the developed world:

1. Australia: The Royal Children's Hospital in Melbourne was developed through a PPP in 2005. It involved the construction, financing, and maintenance of a new state-of-the-art hospital, which was designed to provide high-quality care to children and their families. The PPP was awarded to a consortium that included construction and financing firms, and the hospital is operated by the Victorian Government.
2. Canada: In Canada, PPPs have been used to build and operate hospitals, diagnostic and treatment centers, and other healthcare facilities. For example, the Saskatchewan government partnered with private companies to build and operate the Regina General Hospital, while the Ontario government partnered with private companies to build and operate the Brampton Civic Hospital.
3. United Kingdom: The United Kingdom has implemented several PPPs in the health sector, particularly in the area of hospital infrastructure. For example, the government has partnered with private companies to build and operate the Royal Liverpool University Hospital and the Midland Metropolitan Hospital.
4. United States: In the United States, PPPs have been used to build and operate hospitals, clinics, and other healthcare facilities. For example, the Los Angeles County government partnered with a private company to build and operate the Martin Luther King Jr. Community Hospital, while the University of California San Francisco Medical Center partnered with a private company to build and operate the UCSF Medical Center at Mission Bay.

Box 12.3 PPPs in the Education Sector in the Developed World

1. **The University of Hertfordshire, UK:** The University of Hertfordshire was developed through a PPP. The project involved the construction of new academic and residential buildings, as well as the provision of facilities management and catering services. The PPP contract was awarded to a consortium consisting of Bouygues UK and its partners.
2. **Nova Scotia Schools, Canada:** In Canada, the province of Nova Scotia, several schools have been built and maintained through PPPs. The PPP contracts include the design, construction, financing, and maintenance of the schools over a period of 30 years. The PPP contracts were awarded to consortia consisting of private sector firms and public sector entities.
3. **Limerick Institute of Technology, Ireland:** In Ireland, the Limerick Institute of Technology was developed through a PPP. The project involved the construction of a new campus building, as well as the provision of facilities management and maintenance services. The PPP contract was awarded to a consortium consisting of BAM Building and its partners.
4. **University of Toronto, Canada:** In Canada, the University of Toronto has used PPPs to develop student housing. The PPP contracts include the design, construction, financing, and maintenance of the housing over a period of 30 years.
5. **City College Norwich, UK:** In the UK, City College Norwich was developed through a PPP. The project involved the construction of a new campus building, as well as the provision of facilities management and catering services. The PPP contract was awarded to a consortium consisting of Morgan Sindall Investments and its partners.

- ***Health:*** The healthcare sector is the second most common sector for PPPs in the developed world, accounting for around 10% of all PPP projects in OECD countries. A study by the UK National Audit Office found that PPPs for healthcare facilities in the UK have led to improved patient satisfaction and shorter waiting times. PPPs in healthcare have been used for the construction and operation of hospitals, clinics, and other healthcare facilities.

- ***Education Sector:*** PPPs have also been common in the education sector in the developed world, and are mainly involved in the construction and operation of schools, universities, and other educational facilities. In the United States, between 2000 and 2016, there were a total of 151 PPPs in the education sector, with a total investment value of $23.9 billion. In the United Kingdom, PPPs have been used extensively in the education sector since the 1990s. As of 2019, there were more than 500 PPP projects in the education sector, with a total value of over £11 billion. In Australia, PPPs have been used in the education sector since the early 2000s. As of 2018,

Box 12.4 PPPs in Water and Wastewater Management in the Developed World

1. **Thames Water**: Thames Water is the largest water and wastewater services company in the UK. It operates under a PPP model where private investors own and operate the infrastructure while the government regulates the industry. This PPP model has been in place since the late 1980s and has been successful in providing efficient and cost-effective water and wastewater services to customers in the UK.
2. **Melbourne Water:** Melbourne Water is a water and wastewater services company that operates in the state of Victoria in Australia. The company was established through a PPP model in the mid-1990s, where private investors own and operate the infrastructure while the government regulates the industry. This PPP model has been successful in improving the quality of water and wastewater services in Melbourne and reducing the impact of water-related hazards, such as floods.
3. **Kwinana Desalination Plant:** The Kwinana Desalination Plant is a water treatment plant located in Western Australia. It was developed through a PPP model, where a private consortium designed, built, and operates the plant under a long-term contract with the government.
4. **Southern Seawater Desalination Plant**: The Southern Seawater Desalination Plant is a water treatment plant located in Western Australia. It was also developed through a PPP model, where a private consortium designed, built, and operates the plant under a long-term contract with the government.

there were a total of 22 PPPs in the education sector, with a total value of AUD 4.4 billion.

- ***Water and Wastewater Management:*** PPPs are prevalent in the water and wastewater management sector of developed countries. They facilitate the construction and operation of essential infrastructure like treatment plants, resulting in 186 PPPs during 2000 to 2016 with a total investment value of $64.6 billion in the United States alone. PPPs have been extensively prevalent in the waste management sector of the United Kingdom since 1990s, with over 60 projects valued at £10 billion as of 2019. In Australia and Canada, PPPs are employed in water and wastewater sectors since early 2000s; there are a total of 24 PPP projects worth AUD 9.5 billion and 20 PPP initiatives with CAD 2.2 billion investment value, respectively (as per data till year-end 2018).
- **Energy:** PPPs have become a common approach in the energy sector for developing and managing power plants, transmission lines, and other essential infrastructure. In the United States alone, 74 PPPs were executed from 2000 to 2016 with an overall investment of $17.7 billion. The UK has also extensively utilized PPPs within its energy sector since the 1990s, resulting in over £50 billion invested across more than 100 projects as of 2019. Additionally, Australia and Canada have both implemented numerous PPP projects worth AUD 9.7 billion and CAD 3.6 billion, respectively, by the end of 2018 focused on enhancing their respective energy sectors from early 2000 onward.

Box 12.5 PPPs in the Energy Sector in the Developed World

1. **London Array Offshore Wind Farm—United Kingdom:** This PPP project involved the development of a 175-turbine offshore wind farm in the Thames Estuary.
2. **Ivanpah Solar Electric Generating System—United States:** This PPP project involved the development of a 392 MW solar thermal power plant in the Mojave Desert of California.
3. **Port Augusta Renewable Energy Park—Australia**: This PPP project involved the development of a 375 MW renewable energy park in South Australia, which includes wind, solar, and battery storage facilities.
4. **Niagara Tunnel Project—Canada:** This PPP project involved the construction of a 10.2 km tunnel to divert water from the Niagara River to a hydroelectric power plant.

PPPs in the Developing World

PPPs are not less prevalent in developing countries compared to developed countries. In fact, PPPs are becoming increasingly popular in many developing countries as a means to attract private investment and expertise to support infrastructure development and service delivery. Many developing countries face significant infrastructure gaps, such as inadequate transportation networks, insufficient power generation capacity, and limited access to clean water and sanitation. PPPs provide an avenue for governments to leverage private sector resources to address these gaps, while also sharing risks and responsibilities with private partners. Here are some examples of PPPs in various sectors in the developing world:

Box 12.6 Examples of PPP Projects in the Infrastructure Sector in the Developing World

1. The Mactan-Cebu International Airport in Philippines was developed through a PPP. The project involved the construction of a new airport terminal and the operation and maintenance of the airport.
2. Lagos-Ibadan Expressway, Nigeria: This PPP involved the rehabilitation and expansion of a major highway in Nigeria, the Lagos-Ibadan Expressway. The project was led by the government-owned company Nigerian Sovereign Investment Authority (NSIA), with private sector partners including Julius Berger Nigeria and RCC Nigeria.
3. Lima Metro, Peru: This PPP involved the construction and operation of a new rapid transit system in the city of Lima, Peru. The project was delivered under a concession agreement between the government of Peru and private sector consortium Metro de Lima Línea 2.
4. Mombasa Water Supply and Sanitation Project, Kenya: This PPP involved the provision of water supply and sanitation services in the city of Mombasa, Kenya. The project was led by the government-owned company Athi Water Services Board, with private sector partners including water utility firm Biwater and investment firm Actis.

Infrastructure: PPPs have been prevalent in the developing world to finance and develop infrastructure such as roads, bridges, airports, and ports. In India, between 1991 and 2017, there were a total of 1449 PPP projects in the infrastructure sector, with a total investment value of $225.4 billion. In Brazil, between 1990 and 2018, there were a total of 1004 PPP projects in the infrastructure sector, with a total investment value of $381.9 billion. In China, between 1984 and 2018, there were a total of 6007 PPP projects in the infrastructure sector, with a total investment value of $3.1 trillion. In Mexico, between 1992 and 2018, there were a total of 250 PPP projects in the infrastructure sector, with a total investment value of $53.9 billion.

Water and sanitation: PPPs in the water and sanitation sector in the developing world have offered opportunities to improve service delivery and attract private investment. However, they also face challenges related to inadequate infrastructure, social and political instability, and tariff adjustments. Here are some examples:

1. ***Manila Water Company, Philippines:*** In 1997, the Philippine government entered into a 25-year concession agreement with the Manila Water Company for the provision of water and wastewater services in the eastern part of Metro Manila. The concessionaire was responsible for expanding and improving water supply and wastewater treatment services in the area, while the government retained ownership of the assets.
2. ***Dar es Salaam Water and Sewerage Authority, Tanzania***: In 2003, the Tanzanian government entered into a ten-year lease agreement with a private company, City Water Services, for the provision of water and wastewater services in Dar es Salaam. The PPP aimed to improve the efficiency and effectiveness of service delivery through private sector participation. However, the PPP faced challenges related to inadequate infrastructure, high levels of non-revenue water, and tariff adjustments.
3. ***La Paz and El Alto Water and Sanitation Company, Bolivia:*** In 1997, the Bolivian government entered into a concession agreement with Aguas del Illimani, a consortium of private companies, for the provision of water and sanitation services in La Paz and El Alto. The PPP aimed to improve service quality, increase access to water and sanitation services, and attract private investment.

However, the PPP faced challenges related to social unrest, political instability, and opposition from civil society groups.

4. ***Nairobi City Water and Sewerage Company, Kenya:*** In 2001, the Kenyan government entered into a lease agreement with a private company, City Water Services, for the provision of water and sanitation services in Nairobi.

Healthcare: PPPs in the health sector in the developing world have been implemented to address the challenges faced by public health systems in many countries, such as inadequate infrastructure, limited resources, and insufficient access to healthcare services. Here are some examples:

1. The ***Aravind Eye Care System in India*** operates under a PPP model, where it provides affordable eye care services to the rural poor.
2. ***Primary healthcare centers in Nigeria:*** In Nigeria, the government has partnered with private providers to deliver primary healthcare services in rural areas. These partnerships have focused on improving access to basic healthcare services and reducing the burden on public health facilities.
3. ***Cancer treatment centers in Brazil:*** In Brazil, the government has implemented PPPs to establish specialized cancer treatment centers in underserved areas. The partnerships have focused on providing high-quality cancer care, including prevention, diagnosis, treatment, and support services.
4. ***HIV/AIDS prevention and treatment programs in South Africa:*** In South Africa, PPPs have been established to address the country's HIV/AIDS epidemic. The partnerships have focused on improving access to prevention, testing, treatment, and care services for people living with HIV/AIDS.

Education: PPPs in the education sector in the developing world are less common than in other sectors, such as transportation and energy. However, some examples of PPPs in the education sector in the developing world include:

1. ***Bridge International Academies, Kenya:*** Bridge International Academies is a private company that operates a network of low-cost

private schools in Kenya, Uganda, Nigeria, and India. The company works in partnership with governments and local communities to provide quality education to low-income families.

2. ***Punjab Education Foundation, Pakistan:*** The Punjab Education Foundation is a government-owned organization that works in partnership with private schools to provide free education to children from low-income families in Punjab, Pakistan.
3. ***Edupreneur Village Fund, India:*** The Edupreneur Village Fund is a social impact fund that invests in education technology start-ups in India. The fund provides financing, mentoring, and networking opportunities to help these start-ups scale their businesses and improve education outcomes.
4. ***Programa de Educación Comunitaria de Tiempo Extendido, Mexico:*** The Programa de Educación Comunitaria de Tiempo Extendido (PEC) is a government program in Mexico that works in partnership with private organizations to provide after-school education programs to children in low-income communities.

Energy: PPPs in the energy sector help to attract private investment and expertise, while also provide much-needed energy infrastructure and services in developing countries. However, these projects face unique challenges related to regulatory frameworks, political and economic stability, and technical capacity. Here are some examples:

1. ***Azura-Edo Power Plant, Nigeria:*** This PPP involved the construction and operation of a 459 MW gas-fired power plant in Nigeria. The project was developed by a private consortium, Azura Power West Africa, and the Nigerian government, with support from the International Finance Corporation (IFC).
2. ***La Virgen Solar Power Plant, Chile:*** This PPP involved the construction and operation of a 69 MW solar power plant in Chile. The project was developed by a private consortium, SunPower Corporation and Total SA, in partnership with the Chilean government.
3. ***Jhimpir Power Plant, Pakistan:*** This PPP involved the construction and operation of a 50 MW wind power plant in Pakistan. The project was developed by a private consortium, Fauji Foundation, and the Pakistani government, with support from the Asian Development Bank (ADB).

4. ***Olkaria Geothermal Power Plant, Kenya:*** This PPP involved the expansion of an existing geothermal power plant in Kenya. The project was developed by a private consortium, OrPower4 Inc., and the Kenyan government, with support from the IFC.

I. **Overview of PPPs in Pakistan**

History and Evolution

PPPs in Pakistan have a relatively short history, dating back to the early 1990s. The country's first PPP project was initiated in 1991, when the government of Punjab Province entered into a contract with a private firm to build and operate a toll road between Lahore and Sheikhupura.

However, it wasn't until the early 2000s that PPPs began to gain more momentum in Pakistan. In 2001, the government of Pakistan launched its first policy framework for PPPs, with the aim of attracting private investment in infrastructure development. This framework established the legal and regulatory framework for PPPs, outlining the procedures and criteria for selecting private sector partners and developing PPP projects.

In recent years, Pakistan has witnessed a growing adoption of PPPs for the development of diverse infrastructure initiatives such as highways, airports, power generation facilities, and water treatment plants alongside educational institutions. Additionally, PPPs have been utilized to deliver social services encompassing healthcare provisions and affordable housing arrangements in the country.

Pakistan has made significant efforts to enhance the environment for PPPs by implementing various measures. This includes establishing specific units within government ministries that facilitate PPP projects, creating a center of excellence for PPPs to offer training and capacity building opportunities, and introducing innovative financing mechanisms aimed at drawing in private investment. These constructive steps signify Pakistan's unwavering commitment toward promoting mutually beneficial partnerships between public entities and private investors, which could pave the way for sustainable economic growth in the country.

Legal and Regulatory Framework

The legal and regulatory framework for PPPs in Pakistan is established by a combination of laws, policies, and guidelines at the federal and provincial levels. Here are some of the key elements of this framework:

1. ***Public-Private Partnership Authority (P3A)***

Initially, there was an Infrastructure Project Development Facility (IPDF), formed in 2006 at the federal level for the facilitation of PPPs. Since the mandate of IPDF was restricted only to the capacity building and advisory services, therefore, it was replaced in 2017 with the Public-Private Partnership Authority (P3A) under the PPP Authority Act, 2017, which was subsequently amended through 2022 Amendment Act. The provisions of P3A Act, 2022, are applicable at the federal level and the functions of P3A are limited only to the infrastructure and power projects.

2. ***The National PPP Policy Framework 2019***

This policy document provides guidelines for the development of PPP projects in Pakistan, and outlines the government's objectives and priorities for PPPs.

3. ***The Public Procurement Regulatory Authority (PPRA) Rules***

The PPRA is responsible for regulating the procurement of goods, works, and services by public sector entities in Pakistan. The PPRA Rules provide guidance on the selection of private sector partners for PPP projects, including the use of competitive bidding processes.

4. ***Provincial PPP Laws and Policies***

The infrastructure and social service needs of the provinces outpace the provincial fiscal space that is currently available for new infrastructure investments. Therefore, just like federation, provinces have their own regulatory bodies dealing with several PPP projects. These regulatory bodies are involved in projects which come under the jurisdiction of provinces.

Punjab has Punjab Public-Private Partnership Authority (PPPPA) established in 2019 under Punjab PPP Act, 2019. Sindh—third largest province by size and second largest province by population—also has a public-private partnership unit working under Sindh Finance Department. KP and Baluchistan also have their PPP units under their Planning and Development Departments.

Box 12.7 Public Private Partnership (PPP) Act, 2017

The Public-Private Partnership (PPP) Act 2017 in Pakistan is a comprehensive legal framework that outlines the following key features:

PPP Authority: The Act establishes the PPP Authority as the main regulatory body for PPPs in Pakistan. The PPP Authority is responsible for developing, implementing, and monitoring PPP projects, as well as conducting feasibility studies, issuing requests for proposals, and negotiating PPP agreements with private sector partners.

Feasibility Studies: The Act requires that all PPP projects be subject to a rigorous feasibility study, which must be approved by the PPP Authority before a project can be initiated. The feasibility study must assess the technical, financial, economic, social, and environmental viability of the project.

Procurement Process: The Act outlines a transparent and competitive procurement process for PPP projects, which includes a public call for proposals, evaluation of proposals based on predetermined criteria, and negotiation and award of the PPP agreement to the successful bidder.

Risk Allocation: The Act provides for a fair allocation of risks between public and private partners, with clear provisions for sharing and managing risks associated with the project.

Dispute Resolution: The Act includes provisions for the resolution of disputes that may arise during the implementation of PPP projects, including the appointment of a dispute resolution committee and the option of arbitration.

Performance Monitoring: The Act requires regular monitoring and evaluation of PPP projects to ensure that they are being implemented in accordance with the terms of the PPP agreement.

Types of PPPs in Pakistan

There are several types of PPPs that are commonly used in Pakistan. Here are some of the main types:

- The most common type of PPP in Pakistan is Build-Operate-Transfer (BOT). Under a BOT arrangement, a private sector partner is responsible for financing, designing, constructing, and operating a project for a set period of time. At the end of the concession period, ownership of the project is transferred back to the public sector partner.
- Under a Build-Own-Operate (BOO) model, a private sector partner is responsible for financing, designing, constructing, and operating a project, with ownership remaining with the private sector partner throughout the concession period.
- The Design-Build-Operate (DBO) model involves a private sector partner being responsible for designing, constructing, and operating a project, but not providing the financing. The public sector partner typically provides the financing for the project.
- The Design-Build-Finance-Operate (DBFO) model is similar to the DBO model, but the private sector partner also provides financing for the project.
- Under a management contract, a private sector partner is responsible for managing and operating a public sector facility, such as a hospital or school, for a set period of time.
- A concession contract is similar to a BOT arrangement, but typically involves a shorter concession period and a greater degree of public sector involvement in the project.
- Under a joint venture, the public and private sector partners form a partnership to develop and operate a project. Ownership and financing responsibilities are typically shared between the partners.

National Evidence on PPPs in Pakistan

The national evidence of PPPs in Pakistan has shown that when implemented effectively, PPPs can be successful in achieving their intended objectives. Over the years, several PPP projects have been undertaken in the country, ranging from transportation and energy infrastructure to healthcare and education services Abdul, R. (2006). Here are some examples:

Energy Sector: The energy/power sector in Pakistan is one of the major areas where PPPs are common. According to PPP Monitor, 2021, of Asian Development Bank, the number of projects completed under PPP from 1990–2019 have been 108 with an investment of $28.4 billion. More than 80% ($ 24.7 billion) of these projects have been in the energy sector. According to P3A, as of September 2021, there are 36 ongoing PPP projects in the energy sector with a total investment of around USD 12.6 billion. These projects include power generation, transmission, and distribution. Here are some examples:

Power Generation Projects: Several power generation projects have been developed through PPPs, including coal-fired, gas-fired, and renewable energy projects. For instance, the 1320 MW Port Qasim Coal-fired Power Plant in Karachi and the 50 MW Jhimpir Wind Power Project in Sindh were both developed under PPP arrangements.

Transmission and Distribution Projects: PPPs have also been involved in developing transmission and distribution projects to improve the efficiency and reliability of the energy grid. For example, the Transmission Line for Wind Power Projects in Sindh was developed through a PPP arrangement.

Renewable Energy Projects: There is a growing focus on renewable energy in Pakistan, and many PPP projects have been launched in this area. For instance, the Quaid-e-Azam Solar Power Park in Bahawalpur was developed through a PPP arrangement, which has a total capacity of 1000 MW.

Apart from the energy sector, PPPs also work in other areas as well including transportation, health, education, and water, and sanitation.

Health: PPPs in healthcare involve collaborations between the government and private sector entities to improve access to quality healthcare services. In Pakistan, the government has initiated several PPP projects in the health sector, such as the establishment of primary healthcare facilities in rural areas, public-private partnerships for the provision of diagnostic and treatment services, and collaborations for the development of medical education and training facilities Nurkaeva & Irina (2022), Smyshlyaev (2022). One of the most significant PPP projects in the health sector is the Sehat Sahulat Program, which is a health insurance scheme launched by the government in collaboration with private insurance companies. The program aims to provide free health coverage to the underprivileged sections of society, including those living below the poverty line and those with disabilities. Another example of PPPs in the health sector in Pakistan is the establishment of telemedicine centers, which provide remote medical consultation and treatment to patients living in remote areas. The government has partnered with private sector entities to establish and run these centers, which have helped to improve access to healthcare services for people living in underserved areas.

Education: The Government of Pakistan has launched several initiatives to encourage private sector involvement in education, including PPPs. One of the major PPP initiatives in the education sector in Pakistan is the Public-Private Partnership Support Facility (PPPSF), which was established in 2010 by the Ministry of Finance. The facility aims to facilitate PPP projects in various sectors, including education.

The PPPSF has supported several PPP projects in the education sector, including the establishment of the Lahore University of Management Sciences (LUMS) and the National University of Technology (NUTECH). Both universities are operated by private sector organizations under PPP arrangements with the Government of Pakistan.

In addition to universities, the government of Pakistan has also encouraged private sector involvement in the construction and management of public schools under PPP arrangements. For example, the Punjab Education Foundation (PEF) has established a PPP program to improve the quality of education in public schools in Punjab province. The program involves partnering with private sector organizations to construct and manage schools, with the government providing funding and oversight.

Transportation Sector: One of the major PPP initiatives in the transportation sector in Pakistan is the China-Pakistan Economic Corridor (CPEC), which is a multi-billion dollar infrastructure development project. The CPEC includes several transportation infrastructure projects, such as the construction of highways, railways, and ports. These projects are being developed through PPP arrangements with Chinese companies and the Government of Pakistan.

In addition to the CPEC, the Government of Pakistan has also utilized PPPs to develop other transportation infrastructure projects. For example, the Lahore Ring Road was developed through a PPP arrangement between the government of Punjab and a private consortium. The project involved the construction of a 42 km long expressway to bypass Lahore City and connect various highways.

The Government of Pakistan has also encouraged private sector involvement in the development of public transportation systems, such as bus rapid transit (BRT) systems. The Peshawar BRT project, for example, was developed through a PPP arrangement between the government of Khyber Pakhtunkhwa and a private consortium. The project involved the construction of a BRT system in Peshawar city, which has significantly improved public transportation services in the area.

Another major PPP initiative in the transportation sector in Pakistan is the National Highway Authority's (NHA) PPP program. Initially, it had been a government-run agency which became successful after partnering with the private companies. Under this program, private sector companies are invited to finance, design, construct, operate, and maintain highways and motorways in Pakistan. The NHA has already awarded several PPP contracts for the development of transportation infrastructure in the country.

The Government of Pakistan has also used PPPs to develop public transportation systems. For example, the Lahore Metro Bus System is a PPP project in which the Government of Punjab partnered with a private company to develop and operate a rapid transit bus system in Lahore. Similarly, the Karachi Circular Railway project is another PPP project that aims to revive the city's circular railway system.

Furthermore, the Government of Pakistan has also used PPPs to develop and operate airports in the country, such as the New Islamabad International Airport, which was developed and is being operated through a PPP arrangement with a private consortium.

Case Studies of Successful PPPs in Pakistan

Lahore Ring Road Project: This PPP project involved the construction of a 35-kilometer, 6-lane ring road around Lahore. The project was completed ahead of schedule and under budget, and has significantly reduced traffic congestion in the city.

Jamshoro Power Plant: This PPP project involved the construction of a 1200-megawatt coal-fired power plant in Sindh Province. The project has helped to alleviate the country's chronic power shortages and has contributed to economic growth.

Faisalabad Industrial Estate Development and Management Company (FIEDMC): This PPP project involved the development of an industrial estate in Faisalabad. The project has created jobs and attracted significant investment to the region.

Lahore University of Management Sciences (LUMS): LUMS has become one of the top universities in the country and has produced a generation of highly skilled graduates.

Lahore Metro Bus System: The Lahore Metro Bus System is a public transport system built through a PPP model. It is jointly owned by the Punjab government and a private company, and the buses are operated and maintained by the private sector. The system has improved public transport in Lahore and reduced congestion on the city's roads.

Examples of Failed PPP Projects in Pakistan

The success of the PPPs in Pakistan can be attributed to several factors, including the establishment of a robust legal and regulatory framework, transparent procurement processes, effective risk allocation mechanisms, and strong government support. However, challenges such as lack of transparency, inadequate risk assessment, and issues with contract management have also been encountered in some cases which led to the failure of PPP projects. There are some examples of PPP failures in Pakistan.

One example is the Lahore Waste Management Company, which was established as a PPP to improve waste management in the city of Lahore. However, the project faced challenges due to issues such as insufficient funds, lack of technical expertise, and resistance from the informal waste sector. As a result, the Lahore Waste Management Company was unable to achieve its objectives, and the waste management situation in the city remains poor.

Another example of a PPP failure in Pakistan is the Lahore Rapid Mass Transit System (LRMTS), which was supposed to be a metro train project in Lahore. The project was launched as a PPP, but it faced numerous delays and cost overruns due to various reasons such as land acquisition issues, legal challenges, and disagreements between the government and private sector partners. Eventually, the Government of Punjab had to take over the project, and it is now being developed as a government-funded project.

These failures highlight the importance of proper planning, risk assessment, and monitoring in PPP projects, as well as the need for the government to maintain a balance between attracting private investment and ensuring protection of public interests.

Box 12.8 Loopholes in the PPPs Legal Framework
The PPPs Act, 2017, is the regulatory framework for Public-Private Partnership (PPP) projects in Pakistan. While the Act aims to provide a legal and regulatory framework for PPPs, there are concerns about certain loopholes that could potentially undermine the effectiveness of the Act. Here are some examples of potential loopholes in the PPPs Act, 2017, in Pakistan:

Ambiguity in the definition of PPPs: The definition of PPPs in the Act is broad and vague, which could lead to confusion about what types of projects fall under the scope of the Act.

Limited scope of applicability: The Act only applies to projects that are deemed to be of "national importance," which could limit its applicability and effectiveness in promoting PPPs in other sectors.

Lack of clear criteria for project selection: The Act does not provide clear criteria for selecting projects for PPPs, which could lead to potential bias or unfair practices in the selection process.

Limited transparency and accountability: The Act does not mandate sufficient disclosure and transparency in the selection and implementation of PPP projects, which could lead to potential corruption or mismanagement.

Inadequate risk allocation: The Act does not provide sufficient guidance on how risks should be allocated between the public and private sectors in PPP projects, which could lead to disputes and potential losses for the public sector.

These loopholes could potentially undermine the effectiveness of the PPPs Act, 2017, in promoting PPP projects in Pakistan. Therefore, it is essential for the government and relevant stakeholders to address these issues and strengthen the regulatory framework to ensure transparency, accountability, and effective risk allocation in PPP projects.

Challenges Faced by PPPs in Pakistan

While PPPs can bring many benefits to infrastructure development and service delivery, there are also a number of challenges that can arise during their implementation. In the context of Pakistan, here are some of the challenges that PPPs have faced:

Political Instability: Political instability poses a major challenge to the PPPs in Pakistan, as changes in government or policy disrupt the continuity of projects and undermine investor confidence.

Procurement and Contracting: The procurement and contracting process for PPP projects in Pakistan is lengthy and cumbersome, which discourages potential investors and increases project costs.

Risk Allocation: The allocation of risk between public and private partners can be a major challenge in PPPs. In Pakistan, the risk allocation process has been complicated and unclear, which creates uncertainty for investors.

Financing: Access to financing can be a major challenge for PPP projects in Pakistan, particularly in sectors with high capital costs such as infrastructure. This makes it difficult to attract private sector partners and increases the burden on the public sector.

Capacity Constraints: The public sector in Pakistan lacks the technical expertise and capacity needed to effectively manage PPP projects, which has led to delays and increased costs in many instances.

Social and Environmental Issues: PPP projects in Pakistan may face social and environmental challenges, such as land acquisition issues, community opposition, and environmental concerns, which can increase project costs and delays.

Legal and Regulatory Framework: While Pakistan has a legal and regulatory framework for PPPs, it is still evolving and is complex and bureaucratic, which leads to delays and uncertainty in project implementation.

These challenges have affected many PPP projects in the country. Here are a few examples:

Lahore Orange Line Metro Train Project: The Lahore Orange Line Metro Train Project faced significant challenges related to political instability, legal and regulatory framework, procurement and contracting, and financing. The project was delayed due to changes in government and political opposition, and the procurement and contracting process was criticized for being opaque and inefficient. Additionally, the project faced financing challenges due to its high cost, with some investors being hesitant to participate.

Karachi Water and Sewerage Services Improvement Project: The Karachi Water and Sewerage Services Improvement Project faced challenges related to capacity constraints and risk allocation. The project was designed to improve water and sewerage services in the city, but was delayed due to the lack of technical expertise and capacity in the public sector to manage the project effectively. Additionally, the allocation of risk between the public and private partners was unclear, leading to disputes and delays in implementation.

Sukkur-Multan Motorway Project: The Sukkur-Multan Motorway Project faced challenges related to social and environmental issues. The project involved the construction of a motorway through agricultural land and villages, which led to protests from affected communities. Additionally, there were concerns about the potential environmental impact of the project, particularly in terms of the loss of agricultural land and the displacement of local communities.

Concluding Remarks

A detailed discussion on the PPPs scenario in the whole world and in Pakistan, we sum up that PPPs success in Pakistan requires careful planning and implementation.

A transparent procurement process is critical for the success of PPPs. The process should be fair, competitive, and transparent. All stakeholders should be involved in the procurement process, and there should be clear guidelines for evaluating bids. Main advantages of this successful PPPs are the ability to allocate risks between the public and private sectors. Effective risk allocation is essential for the success of PPPs. Risks should be allocated to the party which is best equipped to manage them. Risks should be identified and quantified upfront, and appropriate risk mitigation measures should be put in place. The financing structure should also be sustainable, and should allow for the sharing of risks and returns between the public and private sectors. Moreover, effective management practices must be promoted that could in running successful PPPs and can bring significant benefits if carefully planned, implemented, and managed.

References

Abdul, R. (2006). Public-private investment linkage in Pakistan: A multivariate cointegration analysis. *South Asia Economic Journal*. https://doi.org/10.1177/139156140600700204

Anas, M., Amit, Y., Aquib, A., Anand, K. S., & Maaz, A. K. (2017). Financial modeling of public private partnership in wastewater treatment. *International Journal of Advance Research, Ideas and Innovations in Technology, 3*(6).

Arpita, T. (2022). Public-private partnerships: A dynamic discrete choice model for road projects. *Socio-economic Planning Sciences*. https://doi.org/10.1016/j.seps.2022.101227

Bilal, A., Muhammad, I. A., Aftab, A. (2018). Opportunities and risk factors in public-private partnership on energy: A critical analysis of solar photovoltaic plant at bahawalpur. https://doi.org/10.31703/GPR.2018(III-II).07

Nurkaeva, A., & Irina, V. (2022). Development of health infrastructure on the basis of using the mechanism of public-private partnership. Vestnik Altajskoj akademii èkonomiki i prava. https://doi.org/10.17513/vaael.2509

Smyshlyaev, A. V. (2022). Public-private partnership in the system of compulsory health insurance: Features and trends. Spravočnik vrača obŝej praktiki. https://doi.org/10.33920/med-10-2206-02

PART V

Political Economy of Privatization

CHAPTER 13

Political Economy of Privatization

Abstract The privatization process in Pakistan has been highly contentious, marked by allegations of corruption, cronyism, and political influence. While some argue that privatization has led to improved efficiency and performance of formerly state-owned enterprises, others argue that the process has been marred by political interference and has failed to deliver the promised benefits. This chapter examines the political economy of privatization in Pakistan, focusing on the role of political institutions, interest groups, and rent-seeking behavior in shaping the privatization process, as well as the social and economic implications of privatization for the Pakistani people. Through a detailed analysis of specific privatization case studies like PTCL, MCB, PSM, UBL, DISCOs, and PIA, this chapter aims to shed light on the complex and often fraught relationship between politics and economic policy in Pakistan.

Keywords Cronyism in Privatization • Political Interference in Privatization • Privatization Benefits • Political Economy • Role of Political Institutions • Rent-seeking

G. Samad, N. Faraz, *The Face of Privatization in Pakistan*, https://doi.org/10.1007/978-981-97-8385-4_13

Role of Actors in Shaping the Privatization Process of Pakistan

Political institutions in Pakistan have played a significant role in shaping the privatization process. The government has taken the lead in initiating and executing privatization policies. The role of the parliament has been critical in terms of providing a legislative framework for privatization, approving the sale of SOEs, and overseeing the implementation of privatization policies. However, the government's political interests have often influenced the timing and execution of privatization programs.

Interest groups, such as labor unions and political parties, have been important actors in shaping the privatization process in Pakistan. Labor unions have been the most significant opponents of privatization in Pakistan. They have organized protests, strikes, and other forms of resistance to privatization, citing concerns about job security and the welfare of workers. Political parties in Pakistan have also opposed privatization, both for ideological reasons and political gain. Some parties view privatization as a neoliberal policy that benefits only the rich and powerful, while others see it as a threat to national sovereignty and security. Political opposition to privatization has been particularly strong when it comes to the sale of strategic assets, such as Pakistan International Airlines (PIA), which has been the subject of much political debate and controversy.

Rent-seeking behavior has also been a significant factor in shaping the privatization process in Pakistan. Rent-seeking refers to the practice of using one's position of power to extract economic rents or benefits. Privatization can create opportunities for rent-seeking, as powerful actors seek to gain control of state-owned enterprises for their own economic gain. For example, there have been instances in Pakistan where privatization has been used as a means of rewarding political allies or insiders, rather than pursuing economic efficiency.

The role of donor agencies was also a significant factor in the privatization of SOEs in Pakistan. Since 1990s, Pakistan has been receiving loans and aid packages from various donor agencies, including the World Bank, the Asian Development Bank, and the International Monetary Fund (IMF). Apart from financial assistance, these agencies provided technical support, and established the regulatory framework for the privatization process. However, while the role of donor agencies may have been crucial, it was not the only reason for privatization in Pakistan.

The role of the judiciary in privatization in Pakistan has been significant, especially in ensuring transparency and fairness in the privatization process. The judiciary has intervened in many cases where the privatization process was deemed to be corrupt or illegal, and has ordered the cancellation of several privatization deals in the past. One of the most significant cases in which the judiciary intervened was the privatization of Pakistan Steel Mills (PSM). In 2006, the government had sold PSM to a Saudi consortium, but the sale was later challenged in court on the grounds of corruption and lack of transparency. The Supreme Court of Pakistan ordered the cancellation of the deal in 2009 and directed the government to hold a transparent and competitive bidding process for the privatization of PSM. Similarly, the judiciary has also intervened in several other cases, such as the privatization of PTCL, where the sale was challenged on the grounds of unfair valuation and the non-payment of employee benefits. The Supreme Court ordered the government to address these concerns and ensure that the privatization process was fair and transparent. However, there have been several weaknesses in the judiciary system that have impacted privatization in Pakistan. One of the main weaknesses is the issue of delays in the court system. Cases related to privatization have often been delayed for years, which has caused uncertainty and instability for both the government and investors.

Finally, the political economy of privatization in Pakistan is complicated by a number of structural factors, such as weak regulatory institution and corruption. These factors have often led to privatization being seen as a means for elites to capture public assets and resources for their own benefit, rather than as a tool for economic development and growth.

Instances of Highly Politicized Privatizations in Pakistan

We provide example of some of the privatizations that were embroiled in heated controversies due to their limited competitive nature. These programs were predominantly administered by favored insiders, which further fueled public criticism and scrutiny.

Though Sharif termed his privatization program as "turning Pakistan into a (South) Korea by encouraging greater private saving and investment to accelerate economic growth." However, the privatization of industrial and banking units under the leadership of Prime Minister Nawaz Sharif was characterized by recklessness and favoritism. This approach ultimately led to the rise of a powerful business oligarchy, which has amassed vast amounts of wealth, exacerbating Pakistan's already-significant wealth gap while also contributing to political instability. The process was criticized for being opaque and lacking transparency, with allegations of insider trading, undervaluation of assets, and rigged bidding processes. Some of the most high-profile cases of alleged corruption and favoritism involved the privatization of Muslim Commercial Bank (MCB) and United Bank Limited (UBL).

Muslim Commercial Bank

The privatization of MCB in 1991 was marred by political influence. During the privatization process, there were allegations of corruption and favoritism in the sale of the bank. It was alleged that the sale of MCB was manipulated to favor certain individuals and groups.

The deal was finalized by the government of Prime Minister Nawaz Sharif, where 75% stake was sold to Mian Mansha at a price of 2.42 billion rupees. According to a report by the National Accountability (Ali, 2022) (Khan, 2023), Mansha's consortium was not the highest bidder but it eventually matched the bid offered by the highest bidder. Furthermore, the Sharif family was accused of using offshore companies to acquire the majority stake in MCB during the privatization process. The controversy surrounding the privatization of MCB ultimately led to several legal challenges and inquiries. In 1997, the Supreme Court of Pakistan ordered an investigation into the privatization of MCB, and the subsequent findings confirmed the allegations of corruption and political influence. However, the case was later closed due to lack of evidence, and no one was held accountable for the alleged corruption.

United Bank Limited

The privatization of United Bank Limited (UBL) took place in two phases. The first phase, which started in 1991, involved the sale of a 51% stake in the bank to a consortium of investors led by Saudi businessman Sheikh Nahayan Mabarak Al Nahayan. This consortium included members of the royal family of Abu Dhabi and other prominent individuals from the Gulf region. The sale was completed for a price of $286 million and was considered the largest privatization deal in Pakistan's history at the time.

The second phase of the privatization took place in 2002, when the government sold an additional 26% stake in UBL to the same consortium of investors for $152 million. This brought the total stake held by the consortium to 77%. The remaining 23% stake was offered to the public through the Karachi Stock Exchange. However, there were allegations of preferential treatment toward the consortium in both phases of the privatization, with some claiming that the Sharif family, who were in power at the time, had close personal ties to Sheikh Nahayan and that the sale was rigged to favor the consortium.

Pakistan Steel Mills

The process of privatization of Pakistan Steel Mills was initiated by the government of General Musharraf in 2004. However, the process was fraught with controversies and allegations of wrongdoing. Therefore, it was canceled by the Supreme Court due to irregularities. The process was restarted in 2016 by the government of Prime Minister Nawaz Sharif, but was again mired in controversy and ultimately failed to attract any bidders.

One of the most significant allegations was that the privatization process was rigged to favor a specific bidder, the Russian-led consortium of Magnitogorsk Iron and Steel Works (MMK). It was alleged that the entire process was manipulated to ensure that MMK emerged as the preferred bidder. The MMK consortium had reportedly submitted a low bid, but the privatization authorities allegedly lowered the reserve price to ensure that MMK won the bid.

There were also allegations that the privatization process lacked transparency and accountability. The process was carried out behind closed doors, with little public scrutiny or oversight. The lack of transparency and accountability gave rise to suspicions that the process was being manipulated for personal gain.

Furthermore, it was also alleged that the government had undervalued Pakistan Steel Mills, which resulted in huge losses to the national exchequer. The valuation of Pakistan Steel Mills was a contentious issue throughout the privatization process, and there were claims that the government had deliberately undervalued the company to ensure that it was sold at a lower price.

The political parties in opposition, particularly those with a nationalist agenda, used the privatization of PSM as a political tool to gain public support. They argued that the sale of such a vital national asset to foreign investors would harm Pakistan's sovereignty and economic independence.

Pakistan International Airlines (PIA)

The privatization of PIA, the country's national airline, has also faced significant political pressures and challenges. The process was initiated in 2015 by the government of Prime Minister Nawaz Sharif, but was met with strong opposition from unions, opposition parties, and other stakeholders. The process was subsequently stalled and has yet to be completed.

The government appointed a financial advisory consortium, which included Deutsche Bank, as the lead advisor for the transaction. However, the opposition parties and some experts criticized the government for not conducting the privatization process transparently and for allegedly favoring certain buyers. In 2016, a consortium comprising of Turkish Airlines, Saudi Arabian Airlines, and a local Pakistani company, submitted the highest bid for the 26% stake in PIA. However, the government cancelled the deal following protests by opposition parties and unions representing PIA employees. The government then attempted to revive the privatization process by seeking other buyers, but the efforts did not succeed.

In 2018, the newly elected government of Prime Minister Imran Khan announced that it would not privatize PIA and instead focus on restructuring the airline to make it profitable. The government has since initiated a number of measures to improve the airline's performance, including reducing its debt burden and improving its management and operations. However, PIA continues to face financial and operational challenges, and the government's efforts to turn the airline around have been met with mixed success.

There were arguments made for and against the privatization of PIA, and opinions were divided on whether there was an actual need for privatization. Those in favor of privatization argued that PIA was a loss-making entity that was draining the government's resources, and that it was burdened with inefficiencies, overstaffing, and mismanagement. They argued that privatization would bring in private sector expertise, capital, and efficiency, leading to improved performance, increased profitability, and reduced burden on the taxpayers.

On the other hand, critics of privatization argued that PIA was a strategic asset that had significant economic and social value beyond mere profitability. They argued that privatization would result in job losses, reduced services to remote and less profitable areas, and a decline in the overall quality of services. They also raised concerns about transparency in the privatization process and the potential for corruption.

The critics also raised concerns about the potential security implications of privatizing PIA. They argued that a private owner may prioritize profits over national security, leading to a decline in safety standards and risking Pakistan's aviation industry.

Ultimately, whether there was an actual need for privatization of PIA is a matter of debate and opinion. The government's decision to privatize PIA was based on its assessment of the economic and financial situation of the country, as well as its ideological stance on the role of the government in the economy.

Power Distribution Companies (DISCOs)

The government of Pakistan initiated the privatization of power distribution companies in 2013 with the aim of improving the efficiency and reliability of electricity distribution in the country. Initially, eight power distribution companies were included in the privatization plan, but the process faced delays and only two companies, namely the Faisalabad Electric Supply Company (FESCO) and the Lahore Electric Supply Company (LESCO), were eventually privatized in 2018.

The privatization process for both companies involved the sale of a majority stake to private investors through a competitive bidding process. The successful bidders were the China-based companies, China Guodian Corporation and National Transmission and Despatch Company (NTDC), that formed a joint venture to acquire a 66.4% stake in LESCO and a 74% stake in FESCO.

The privatization of DISCOs in Pakistan was not transparent in several ways. One of the major issues was the lack of transparency in the bidding process. The government failed to provide clear guidelines for the bidding process, which resulted in confusion and a lack of clarity for potential bidders. This lack of transparency gave rise to allegations of favoritism and corruption in the privatization process. According to media reports, some officials of the Privatization Commission and DISCOs were allegedly involved in corrupt practices during the privatization process. It was alleged that some of the bidders were given preferential treatment, while others were denied a fair chance to participate in the bidding process. In particular, there were allegations against former chairman of the Privatization Commission who was accused of irregularities in the privatization process. It was alleged that he favored a group of investors led by Nishat Chunian Power, a company owned by Mian Mansha, a prominent industrialist in Pakistan. The deal was reportedly closed at a much lower price than the market value, leading to accusations of corruption and favoritism.

Moreover, there were also allegations that the bidders were given insider information and were allowed to revise their bids after the deadline, which gave them an unfair advantage over other bidders. It was also alleged that some of the bidders had close connections with politicians and government officials, which helped them to secure the deal.

The privatization of DISCOs has been criticized for several other reasons:

> Critics argue that privatization will lead to an increase in electricity tariffs, making it harder for ordinary consumers to afford electricity. They argue that the private sector is profit-driven, and that the cost of privatization will ultimately be borne by the consumers.

The objective of privatizing DISCOs was to improve the quality of service provided to consumers. However, that has not been achieved in many cases. The companies that acquired DISCOs have failed to make significant investments in infrastructure, resulting in frequent power outages and poor voltage regulation.

Pakistan Telecommunication Company Limited (PTCL)

Pakistan Telecommunication Company Limited (PTCL) was profitable at the time of privatization. In fact, it was one of the most profitable state-owned enterprises in Pakistan. Despite that, the government of Pakistan decided to privatize PTCL because it wanted to reduce its control and involvement in the telecommunications sector and encourage private investment. Although PTCL was profitable, the government believed that privatization would lead to higher levels of investment, better technology, and improved service quality.

The privatization of PTCL was a multi-billion dollar deal that took place in 2006. The government of Pakistan decided to sell a 26% stake in PTCL to a private investor. Etisalat, a telecommunications company based in the United Arab Emirates, won the bid to acquire the stake in PTCL for $2.6 billion. As part of the deal, Etisalat agreed to pay $1.4 billion upfront, while the remaining $1.2 billion was to be paid over the next five years (Rana, 2023).

The privatization of PTCL was widely criticized for being rushed and not in the best interests of the country. The government at the time was accused of selling the company at a low price to a consortium of investors that included Etisalat, a UAE-based company. The deal was also criticized for not including measures to protect the jobs of PTCL employees.

Social and Political Implications of Privatization in Pakistan

The privatization of state-owned enterprises in Pakistan has had significant social and political implications, which have been the subject of ongoing academic debate and scrutiny. Scholars continue to examine how this policy shift has affected various stakeholders, including workers, consumers, government officials, and investors. Through rigorous research and analysis, academics aim to deepen our understanding of the complexities surrounding privatization in Pakistan and inform future policy decisions on this topic. Here are some of the key implications of privatization in Pakistan:

> Privatization has had a significant social impact on employment, particularly in state-owned enterprises that have undergone privatization. The resulting loss of jobs has caused an increase in unemployment and social unrest, specifically among workers directly impacted by the process. According to the International Labor Organization (ILO), around 300,000 workers were laid off in the first wave of privatization during the 1990s in Pakistan. However, there is no consolidated data available on the total number of job losses resulting from privatization in Pakistan as the process has been carried out over a long period and involved various sectors. The actual impact on employment is also subject to debate, as proponents of privatization argue that it has led to the creation of new jobs and increased efficiency in the long run. This demonstrates the complex economic consequences associated with privatizing government-run institutions.

Conclusion

The privatization process in Pakistan is a complex and politically charged issue that has garnered attention from various circles. The decision of the government to initiate the privatization of state-owned enterprises was driven by several factors, such as reducing fiscal burden, boosting economic growth, attracting foreign investment, and enhancing efficiency. However, this process was influenced heavily by political pressures, interest groups' agendas and rent-seeking behavior leading to undesired entities being privatized while necessary ones were not. Privatization offers many advantages if executed properly; hence transparency in this procedure is vital for its success. It must be carried out equitably with inclusivity so that all stakeholders are included regardless of their social status or influence levels. This approach will help ensure that everyone's interests are taken into account throughout the entire transformation period making it successful overall.

References

Ali, S. A. (2022, December 26). *Privatization of Power distribution companies.* Retrieved from The Express Tribune: https://tribune.com.pk/story/2392848/privatisation-of-power-distribution-companies-i

Khan, G. A. (2023, October 15). *Loss-making DISCOs struggle to avoid privatisation.* Retrieved from The Expree Tribune: https://tribune.com.pk/story/2441225/loss-making-discos-struggle-to-avoid-privatisation

Rana, S. (2023, January 26). *Privatisation report fails to mention $800m in dues from Etisalat.* Retrieved from The Express Tribune: https://tribune.com.pk/story/2397784/privatisation-report-fails-to-mention-800m-in-dues-from-etisalat

CHAPTER 14

Way Forward

Abstract This study examines the impact of privatization on SOEs, explained that while privatization has somewhat alleviated the fiscal burden on national resources, it has not significantly enhanced overall performance or efficiency. Through sectoral analysis, it shows that operational efficiency has improved due to better asset utilization, yet results vary across sectors. For example, while compare power, cement, and finance, the cement industry showing notable performance improvements both pre- and post-privatization. The paper advocates for corporate governance reforms, enhanced transparency, and capacity building in government as initial steps toward effective SOE reform. It also highlights the importance of robust legal frameworks and Public-Private Partnerships (PPPs) to ensure the success of privatization efforts, and note them as the essential strategies for achieving a balance between public needs and private sector efficiency.

Keywords Fiscal Burden • SOEs Liabilities • Performance Indicators • Efficiency and Competitiveness • Regulatory Framework • Public-Private Partnerships (PPPs)

The thorough investigation of the SOEs before and after privatization is suggesting that SOEs have proved to be a major burden on the national

G. Samad, N. Faraz, *The Face of Privatization in Pakistan*,
https://doi.org/10.1007/978-981-97-8385-4_14

resources, resulting in a higher fiscal deficit. Though, privatization has resulted in a slight reduction in the fiscal burden, however, the burden remained in the form subsidies and liabilities has not been abolished fully.

An exploratory analysis of the various indicators of performance, efficiency, and competitiveness in various sectors shows a slight improvement in these areas. Empirical analysis also provides robustness that privatization did not bring about big changes in the overall performance of SOEs. However, positive impact on their operational efficiency has been observed considering how well they used their assets to generate returns. Sector-specific case studies of the power sector, cement industry, telecommunications, and financial sector reveal that KE is an ineffective electric utility even after privatization. The financial sector showed better performance, but could not elevate the overall efficiency. The cement industry demonstrated impressive performance both before and after privatization, particularly in terms of capacity, privatization play a minimal role in enhancing the capacity and efficiency of this sector.

Overall, privatization did not play a significant role in achieving the desired outcomes. Thus, as a first step in addressing the issues of SOEs is to address the internal dynamics of SOEs. Corporate governance reforms must be implemented to enhance transparency, accountability, and efficient decision-making. Independent boards and performance-based management become integral to revitalizing these enterprises. Capacity building in the form of investment in the skills and resources of government agencies overseeing SOEs is essential for efficient and transparent processes.

A sound and robust legal and regulatory framework are foundational pillars for the success of privatization initiatives. Such a framework provides clarity, predictability, and fairness, which are essential to attracting private investors and ensuring the credibility of the privatization process. It establishes clear rules for the sale of state-owned assets, safeguards property rights, and enforces contracts, instilling confidence in investors. Additionally, a well-designed regulatory environment can foster competition in industries where privatized entities operate, preventing anti-competitive behavior and ensuring consumer welfare. Furthermore, it serves as a safeguard against corruption and favoritism, promoting transparency and accountability throughout the privatization process. In essence, a strong legal and regulatory framework not only protects the interests of all stakeholders but also creates an environment conducive to efficient, competitive, and successful privatization, ultimately benefiting both the government and the broader economy.

Public-Private Partnerships (PPPs) also come to the forefront. These collaborations leverage private sector expertise and investment while allowing the government to maintain a stake in critical services, striking a balance between public and private interests. PPPs attract private sector investment, relieving the government of the sole financial burden of sustaining SOEs. Private investment can fund infrastructure development, technology upgrades, and capacity expansion, which might have been challenging for SOEs to finance independently. PPPs can result in better service delivery to citizens. Private sector partners are motivated to meet performance targets and provide high-quality services to maintain their reputation and attract future business. Above all, they can enforce fiscal discipline on SOEs, as the private sector is focused on cost-efficiency and profitability. This can help control budgetary pressures and reduce the need for continuous government subsidies.

Appendix A

Data

We rely on firm-level data that covers the pre- and post-privatizaion period of the privatized firms. Since financial and non-financial sector has complete sectoral differences, therefore, we limit our regression analysis to the non-financial firms only that represents more than 90% of the government-owned entities.

We use firms detailed balance sheets which is collected from the State Bank of Pakistan (SBP). In this data set we observe 49 out of 65 government-owned firms which is more 80% of total government-owned firms. We aim to provide pre- versus post-privatization performance, and efficiency of the firms, therefore, we restrict our data to the firms that post profits at least for three years preceding the privatization.[1] Privatization program started in 1991. The data we use in regression analysis starts in 1986 which is five years prior to the first time launch of the privatization in Pakistan.

Our second main dataset covers the privatization transactions from 1991 to 2014. This data comes from the Privatization Commission of Pakistan. This data covers the transactions of all manufacturing, services, and utilities sectors and the privatization year (timing).

[1] We do not have the information for the years 1999 to 2001, as it is not reported by PSEs to the SBP.

G. Samad, N. Faraz, *The Face of Privatization in Pakistan*,
https://doi.org/10.1007/978-981-97-8385-4

Methodology

We use difference-in-difference approach to estimate the effects. We control for the financial and political characteristic to examine the effect of privatization on the performance of PSEs. The regression model is explained as follow:

$$Y_{it} = \propto + \beta Privatize_{it} + \gamma X_{it} + \delta FE + \varepsilon_{it}, \quad (1)$$

where Y_{it} is the performance and efficiency of firm variables that includes the productivity of the firm, sales, net-profits, and rate of returns. $Privatize_{it}$ is the indicator that denote 1 if firm is privatized and 0 otherwise. X_{it} is the vector of control variables, and *FE* are the time-invariants. Prior literature (Dinc & Gupta, 2011) suggests that the firms' financial variables and firm characteristics have a significant impact on the government's decision to privatize firm early or late. This raises concern that, if government is more likely to privatize profitable firms,[2] then comparing the performance of privatized firms to firms that remain government-owned or when they owned by government may overstate the impact of privatization on profitability.

In developing countries, generally, these sales proceeds from privatization flow to government rather than being reinvested in the privatized firms (Megginson, 2005). The government of Pakistan has also used these proceeds to reduce the fiscal deficit rather than reinvested in the other industries. Literature suggests that the privatizing profitable firms first may increase sale proceeds (Megginson et al., 2004; Gupta et al., 2005). In this setting, we observe a positive relationship between the profitability and the privatization decision. On the other hand, literature also suggest that unprofitable enterprises showed a remarkable efficiency improvement in response to privatization. In this setting, we can observe a negative relationship between the profitability and privatization. Hence, the relative importance considered by the government does matter.

Second, the privatization is not popular among the population. It may have political risks for politicians. Politician may avoid this risk by delaying the privatization process. This is widely evident in Pakistan. We bring the political economy of privatization to test the political determinants of the

[2] Tribune October 31, 2018: https://tribune.com.pk/story/1837627/1-11-profitable-entities-shortlisted-sell-off/

privatization. It is widely evident that politicians target public funds to regions with swing voters to win elections. Political connected firms and public enterprises often used to create more jobs in those regions (Cox & McCubbins, 1986; Persson & Tabellini, 2002).

In addition to that, the donors conditionalities effects on privatization in Pakistan. Government often used the fund programs to overcome the economic difficulties. PSEs reforms including the pricing and subsidies, and privatization is one of the fund conditionality (IMF, 2019). This conditionality perhaps can hasten the privatization process without bringing proper reforms (Doyle & Breen, 2013).

Hence, to address these concerns, we run two-stage least square (2SLS) method to measure the effect of privatization on the performance of the firms (results are reported in Table #). Following Gupta and Dinc (2011), in first stage, we use financial and political variables as instruments for the privatization, following Wooldridge (2007), we fit a probit model with Privatize as the dependent variable, we then use the fitted probabilities from this model as an instrument for Privatize in a 2SLS estimation. In second stage, we estimate the Eq. (1) by using the predicted privatization variable to check the impact of the privatization on post-privatization performance. The two-stage estimation reduces the concerns of the selection of firms based on the pre-privatization performance.

Table A.1 Effects of privatization on firm performance

	Δ *in* *Profits/Sales*	Δ *in* *ROA*	Δ *in* *Ln (Sales)*
Stage 2	(1)	(2)	(3)
Privatization	0.865	0.679*	−0.079
	(1.491)	(0.364)	(0.074)
Stage 1			
Lag Ln (Sales)	0.100**	0.098**	0.098**
	(0.412)	(0.382)	(0.382)
Industry FE	Yes	Yes	Yes
Firm FE	Yes	Yes	Yes
State FE	Yes	Yes	Yes
Number of firm-year	1096	884	884

The success of privatization in Pakistan is not clear yet as shown in the figure 6 that industries experience both rise and fall in the fixed assets. In addition, the study of Khan (2004) argues that "in post- privatization period, about only 22% of the privatized units were performing better than in the pre-privatization period, 44% approximately the same and about the third i.e. 34% worse than before."

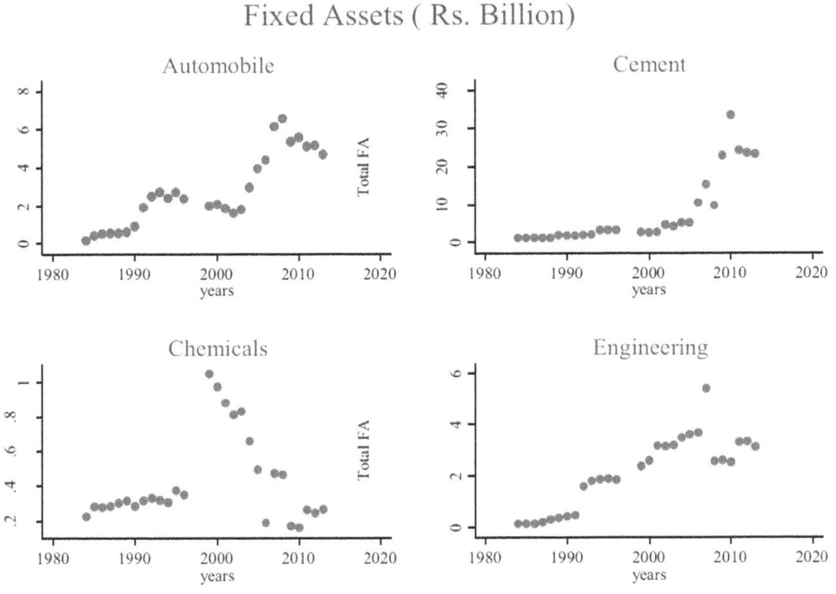

Fig. A.1 Sector-wise fixed assets (in billion PKR)

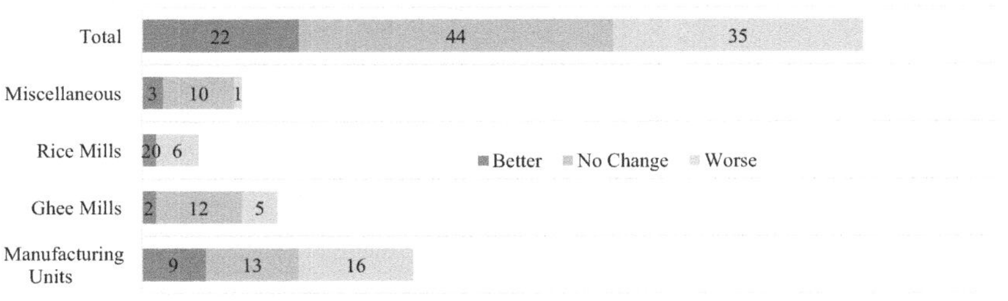

Fig. A.2 First phase post-privatization performance

Appendix B

Table B.1 Evaluation of public versus privatized firms in terms of performance, efficiency, and competitiveness

	Before Privatization		*After Privatization*	
Variables	*Mean*	*Std. Dev*	*Mean*	*Std. Dev*
Performance				
Sales (Rs. million)	4207.21	11419.74	14643.06***	33872.44
Assets (Rs. million)	3449.14	14201.71	6613.23**	24426.81
Net-profits to Sales Ratio	−2.71	29.44	−0.40	2.94
Rate of Return (Net-profits to Assets)	−0.82	4.86	0.29***	2.42
Efficiency				
Sales to Employment Ratio (Efficiency)	0.026	–	0.039	–
Competitiveness				
Concentration ratios	0.54	–	0.35	–
Change in Relative Prices	0.99	–	0.98	–
Fiscal Burden ($US billion)	~$3	–	~$1.8	–
Loans (foreign +Domestic)				
Subsidy				
Observations	320		358	
Number of firms	31	33	33	

G. Samad, N. Faraz, *The Face of Privatization in Pakistan*,
https://doi.org/10.1007/978-981-97-8385-4

Index

G. Samad, N. Faraz, *The Face of Privatization in Pakistan*, https://doi.org/10.1007/978-981-97-8385-4

The manufacturer's authorised representative in the EU is Springer Nature Customer Service Centre GmbH, Europaplatz 3, 69115 Heidelberg, Germany. If you have any concerns regarding our products, please contact ProductSafety@springernature.com

Printed and bound by CPI Group (UK) Ltd, Croydon, CR0 4YY
01/10/2026
02225903-0003